THE TOGAF® STANDARD, VERSION 9.2 – A POCKET GUIDE

The Open Group Publications available from Van Haren Publishing

The TOGAF Series:
The TOGAF® Standard, Version 9.2
The TOGAF® Standard Version 9.2 – A Pocket Guide
TOGAF® 9 Foundation Study Guide, 4th Edition
TOGAF® 9 Certified Study Guide, 4th Edition

The Open Group Series:
The IT4IT™ Reference Architecture, Version 2.1
IT4IT™ for Managing the Business of IT – A Management Guide
IT4IT™ Foundation Study Guide, 2nd edition
The IT4IT™ Reference Architecture, Version 2.1 – A Pocket Guide
Cloud Computing for Business – The Open Group Guide
ArchiMate® 3.0.1 – A Pocket Guide
ArchiMate® 2 Certification – Study Guide
ArchiMate® 3.0.1 Specification

The Open Group Security Series:
O-TTPS - A Management Guide
Open Information Security Management Maturity Model (O-ISM3)
Open Enterprise Security Architecture (O-ESA)
Risk Management – The Open Group Guide
The Open FAIR™ Body of Knowledge – A Pocket Guide

All titles are available to purchase from:
www.opengroup.org
www.vanharen.net
and also many international and online distributors.

The TOGAF®
Standard, Version 9.2

A POCKET GUIDE

Title:	The TOGAF® Standard, Version 9.2 – A Pocket Guide
A publication of:	The Open Group
Authors:	Andrew Josey
	Rachel Harrison
	Paul Homan
	Matthew F. Rouse
	Tom van Sante
	Mike Turner
	Paul van der Merwe
Publisher:	Van Haren Publishing, Zaltbommel, www.vanharen.net
ISBN Hard copy:	978 94 018 0286 4
ISBN eBook (pdf)	978 94 018 0287 1
ISBN eBook EPUB	978 94 018 0288 8
Edition:	First edition, first impression, April 2018
Layout and cover design:	Coco Bookmedia, Amersfoort-NL

The TOGAF® Standard, Version 9.2
A Pocket Guide
Document Number: G185

Published by The Open Group, April 2018.

Comments relating to the material contained in this document may be submitted to:

The Open Group
Apex Plaza
Forbury Road
Reading
Berkshire, RG1 1AX
United Kingdom

or by electronic mail to: ogspecs@opengroup.org

Contents

Preface

This Document

This is the Pocket Guide to the TOGAF® Standard, Version 9.2. It is intended to help architects focus on the efficient and effective operations of their organization and senior managers understand the basics of the TOGAF standard. It is organized as follows:

- Chapter 1 provides a high-level view of the TOGAF standard, Enterprise Architecture, and the contents and key concepts of the standard; it also introduces the TOGAF Library, a portfolio of guidance material supporting the standard
- Chapter 2 provides an introduction to the Architecture Development Method (ADM), the method that the TOGAF standard provides to develop Enterprise Architectures
- Chapter 3 provides an overview of key techniques and deliverables of the ADM cycle
- Chapter 4 provides an overview of the guidelines for adapting the ADM
- Chapter 5 provides an introduction to the Architecture Content Framework, a structured metamodel for architectural artifacts
- Chapter 6 provides an introduction to the Enterprise Continuum, a high-level concept that can be used with the ADM to develop an Enterprise Architecture
- Chapter 7 provides an introduction to the Architecture Capability Framework, a set of resources provided for establishment and operation of an architecture function within an enterprise
- Appendix A provides an overview of the changes between Version 9.1 and Version 9.2 of the TOGAF standard

The audience for this document is:

- Enterprise Architects, Business Architects, IT architects, data architects, systems architects, solutions architects, and senior managers seeking a first introduction to the TOGAF standard

A prior knowledge of Enterprise Architecture is not required. After reading this document, the reader seeking further information should refer to the TOGAF documentation[1] available online at www.opengroup.org/architecture/togaf9-doc/arch and also available as a hardcopy book.

About the TOGAF Standard, Version 9.2

The TOGAF Standard, Version 9.2 is an update to the TOGAF 9.1 Standard providing improved guidance, correcting errors, improving the document structure, and removing obsolete content. Key enhancements made in this version include updates to the Business Architecture and the Content Metamodel. All of these changes make the TOGAF framework easier to use and maintain. It retains the major features and structure of the TOGAF 9.1 Standard including:

Modular Structure: The TOGAF standard has a modular structure. The modular structure supports:
- Greater usability – defined purpose for each part; can be used in isolation as a standalone set of guidelines
- Incremental adoption of the TOGAF standard
- Accompanying the standard is a portfolio of guidance material, known as the TOGAF Library, to support the practical application of the TOGAF approach

Content Framework: The TOGAF standard includes a content framework to drive greater consistency in the outputs that are created when following the Architecture Development Method (ADM). The TOGAF content framework provides a detailed model of architectural work products.

Extended Guidance: The TOGAF standard features an extended set of concepts and guidelines to support the establishment of an integrated

---

1 The TOGAF® Standard, Version 9.2 (C182); refer to www.opengroup.org/library/c182.

hierarchy of architectures being developed by teams within larger organizations that operate within an overarching architectural governance model. In particular, the following concepts are included:

- Partitioning – a number of techniques and considerations on how to partition the various architectures within an enterprise
- Architecture Repository – a logical information model for an Architecture Repository which can be used as an integrated store for all outputs created by executing the ADM
- Capability Framework – a structured definition of the organization, skills, roles, and responsibilities required to operate an effective Enterprise Architecture Capability; the TOGAF Standard also provides guidance on a process that can be followed to identify and establish an appropriate Architecture Capability

Architectural Styles: The TOGAF standard is designed to be flexible and it can be used with various architectural styles. Examples are provided both in the TOGAF standard, in Part III: ADM Guidelines and Techniques, and in the TOGAF Library. Together these comprise a set of supporting materials that show in detail how the ADM can be applied to specific situations; for example:

- The varying uses of iteration that are possible within the ADM and when each technique should be applied
- The various types of architecture development required within an enterprise and how these relate to one another
- The use of the TOGAF ADM with Service-Oriented Architectures (SOAs), Risk and Security, etc.

Additional ADM Detail: The TOGAF Standard, Version 9.2 includes additional detailed information over earlier versions of the TOGAF Standard for supporting the execution of the ADM. Particular areas of enhancement are:

- The Architecture Vision and Business Architecture phases feature extended guidance on development of the Business Architecture;

this includes focus on Business Capabilities, Value Streams, and Organization Maps

- The Technology Architecture phase recognizes that emerging technologies are increasingly leading to technology-driven change

Conventions Used in this Document

The following conventions are used throughout this document in order to help identify important information and avoid confusion over the intended meaning:

- Ellipsis (…)
  Indicates a continuation; such as an incomplete list of example items, or a continuation from preceding text.
- **Bold**
  Used to highlight specific terms.
- *Italics*
  Used for emphasis. May also refer to other external documents.

About The Open Group

The Open Group is a global consortium that enables the achievement of business objectives through technology standards. Our diverse membership of more than 580 organizations includes customers, systems and solutions suppliers, tools vendors, integrators, academics, and consultants across multiple industries.

The Open Group aims to:

- Capture, understand, and address current and emerging requirements, establish policies, and share best practices
- Facilitate interoperability, develop consensus, and evolve and integrate specifications and open source technologies
- Operate the industry's premier certification service

Further information on The Open Group is available at www.opengroup.org.

The Open Group has over 25 years' experience in developing and operating certification programs and has extensive experience developing and facilitating industry adoption of test suites used to validate conformance to an open standard or specification.

The Open Group publishes a wide range of technical documentation, most of which is focused on development of Open Group Standards and Guides, but which also includes white papers, technical studies, certification and testing documentation, and business titles.

A catalog is available at www.opengroup.org/library.

Trademarks

About the Authors

Andrew Josey, The Open Group
Andrew Josey is VP Standards and Certification, overseeing all
certification and testing programs of The Open Group. He also manages
the standards process for The Open Group. At The Open Group, he
has led many standards development projects including specification
and certification development for the ArchiMate®, IT4IT™, TOGAF®,
Open FAIR™, POSIX®, and UNIX® programs. He is a member of the
IEEE, USENIX and the Association of Enterprise Architects (AEA). He
holds an MSc in Computer Science from University College London.

Professor Rachel Harrison, Oxford Brookes University
Rachel Harrison is a Professor of Computer Science in the Department
of Computing and Communication Technologies at Oxford Brookes
University. Previously she was Professor of Computer Science, Head
of the Department of Computer Science, and Director of Research
for the School of Systems Engineering at the University of Reading.
Her research interests include systems evolution, software metrics,
requirements engineering, software architecture, usability and software
testing. She has published over 100 refereed papers and consulted widely
with industry, working with organizations such as IBM, the DERA,
Philips Research Labs, Praxis Critical Systems, and The Open Group.
She is Editor-in-Chief of the Software Quality Journal, published
by Springer. She is the author of the study guides for the TOGAF 9
certification program.

Paul Homan, IBM
Paul Homan is the Chief Technology Officer for Industrial sector
clients within IBM's Global Business Services. He is a Certified Master
IT Architect, specializing in Enterprise Architecture with over 20
years' experience in IT. Highly passionate and practically experienced
in architecture, strategy, design authority, and governance areas,
Paul is particularly interested in Enterprise Architecture leadership,

Requirements Management, and Business Architecture. He joined IBM from end-user environments, having worked as Chief Architect in both the UK Post Office and Royal Mail. He has not only established Enterprise Architecture practices, but has also lived with the results! Since joining IBM, Paul has dedicated his time to both advising clients on Architecture Capability as well as actively leading architecture efforts on large client programs. Paul has also been a leader in building IBM's capability around Enterprise Architecture and the TOGAF framework.

Matthew F. Rouse, DXC Technology
Matthew Rouse is an Enterprise Architect and Deputy Account Chief Technologist at DXC Technology. Matthew has over 20 years' IS/IT experience in applications development, system architecture, IS/IT strategy, and Enterprise Architecture. He brings expertise in strategic IS/IT planning and architecture to ensure that enterprises align their IS/IT investments with their business objectives. Matthew is a Chartered IT Professional member of the British Computer Society, a Master Certified IT Architect, and a member of the IEEE Computer Society.

Tom van Sante, KPN Consulting Nederland
Tom van Sante is a Principal Consultant for KPN Consulting Nederland. He started his career in IT over 30 years ago after studying architecture at the Technical University in Delft. Working in a variety of functions, from operations to management, he has always operated on the borders between business and IT. He was involved in the introduction and development of ITIL/ASL/BiSL in the Netherlands. He has worked in numerous appointments for Government and Industry advising on the use of IT in modern society.

Mike Turner, EY
Mike Turner led Capgemini's development effort on TOGAF Version 9 and also worked in the core team that developed the SAP Enterprise Architecture Framework (a joint initiative between Capgemini and SAP).

He is currently working as Director, Strategy and Architecture Advisory at EY.

Paul van der Merwe, WesBank

Paul van der Merwe is Head of Group Enterprise Architecture, IT Governance, and IT Strategy at WesBank. A conceptual thinker, he has driven a number of advances in the fields in which he has specialized, among them software development, business intelligence, ICT management, and Enterprise Architecture. The fundamental approach to Enterprise Architecture advocated by him is repository-based Enterprise Architecture that should be established within organizations as an ongoing practice that enables business and technology capabilities.

Acknowledgements

The Open Group gratefully acknowledges the following:

- Past and present members of The Open Group Architecture Forum for developing the TOGAF standard
- Capgemini and SAP for contributed materials
- The following reviewers of this and previous editions of this document:
  - Martyn Bowis
  - Corinne Brouch
  - Steve Else
  - Bill Estrem
  - Henry Franken
  - Dave Hornford
  - Judith Jones
  - Henk Jonkers
  - J. Bryan Lail
  - Mike Lambert
  - Kiichiro Onishi
  - Roger Reading
  - Saverio Rinaldi
  - John Rogers
  - Robert Weisman
  - Nicholas Yakoubovsky

Chapter 1
Introduction

This chapter provides an introduction to the TOGAF standard, an open, industry consensus framework for Enterprise Architecture.

Topics addressed in this chapter include:
- An introduction to the TOGAF standard
- The structure and content of the TOGAF documentation
- The kinds of architecture that the TOGAF framework can be used to address

1.1 Introduction to the TOGAF Standard

The TOGAF standard is a framework for Enterprise Architecture. Put simply, it is a standard approach for assisting in the acceptance, production, use, and maintenance of Enterprise Architectures. It is based on an iterative process model supported by best practices and a re-usable set of existing architectural assets.

The TOGAF standard is developed and maintained by members of The Open Group, working within the Architecture Forum. The original development of TOGAF Version 1 in 1995 was based on the US Department of Defense Technical Architecture Framework for Information Management (TAFIM). Starting from this sound foundation, The Open Group Architecture Forum has developed successive versions of TOGAF at regular intervals and published each one on The Open Group public website.

This document covers the TOGAF Standard, Version 9.2, first published in April 2018. It is an update to the TOGAF 9.1 Standard to provide additional guidance, correct errors, address some structural challenges, and remove obsolete content. A description of the changes is provided in Appendix A.

The TOGAF standard can be used for developing a broad range of different Enterprise Architectures. It complements, and can be used in conjunction with, other frameworks that are more focused on specific deliverables for particular vertical sectors such as Government, Telecommunications, Manufacturing, Defense, and Finance. A key part of the TOGAF standard is the method – the TOGAF Architecture Development Method (ADM) – for developing an Enterprise Architecture that addresses business needs.

1.2 Structure of the TOGAF Documentation

The TOGAF documentation consists of the TOGAF standard, and a portfolio of guidance material, known as the TOGAF Library, to support the practical application of the standard.

The TOGAF standard is divided into six parts, as summarized in Table 1.

Table 1: Structure of the TOGAF Standard

Part I: Introduction	This part provides a high-level introduction to the key concepts of Enterprise Architecture and, in particular, to the TOGAF approach. It contains the definitions of terms used throughout the standard.
Part II: Architecture Development Method	This part is the core of the TOGAF framework. It describes the TOGAF Architecture Development Method (ADM) – a step-by-step approach to developing an Enterprise Architecture.
Part III: ADM Guidelines and Techniques	This part contains a collection of guidelines and techniques available for use in applying the TOGAF approach and the TOGAF ADM. Additional guidelines and techniques are also in the TOGAF Library.
Part IV: Architecture Content Framework	This part describes the TOGAF content framework, including a structured metamodel for architectural artifacts, the use of re-usable Architecture Building Blocks (ABBs), and an overview of typical architecture deliverables.
Part V: Enterprise Continuum and Tools	This part discusses appropriate taxonomies and tools to categorize and store the outputs of architecture activity within an enterprise.

| Part VI. Architecture Capability Framework | This part discusses the organization, processes, skills, roles, and responsibilities required to establish and operate an architecture practice within an enterprise. |

Accompanying the standard is the TOGAF Library. The TOGAF Library is a reference library containing guidelines, templates, patterns, and other forms of reference material to accelerate the creation of new architectures for the enterprise. It is structured as summarized in Table 2:

Table 2: Structure of the TOGAF Library

Section 1: Foundation Documents	Broadly applicable information relating to the subject of the TOGAF framework or Enterprise Architecture.
Section 2: Generic Guidance and Techniques	Information describing architecture styles and how the TOGAF framework and Enterprise Architecture can be adapted to exploit the characteristics of a more specific context.
Section 3: Industry-Specific Guidance and Techniques	Information describing how the TOGAF framework and Enterprise Architecture can be applied to meet the specific needs of a vertical industry segment.
Section 4: Organization-Specific Guidance and Techniques	Information describing how the TOGAF framework and Enterprise Architecture have been applied to meet the needs of specific enterprises.

1.3 What is Architecture in the Context of the TOGAF Standard?

ISO/IEC/IEEE 42010:2011[2] defines "architecture" as:

"The fundamental concepts or properties of a system in its environment embodied in its elements, relationships, and in the principles of its design and evolution."

---

2 ISO/IEC/IEEE 42010:2011, Systems and Software Engineering – Architecture Description.

The TOGAF standard embraces but does not strictly adhere to ISO/IEC/IEEE 42010:2011 terminology. In addition to the ISO/IEC/IEEE 42010:2011 definition of "architecture", the TOGAF standard defines a second meaning depending upon the context:

"The structure of components, their inter-relationships, and the principles and guidelines governing their design and evolution over time."

1.4 What kinds of Architecture does the TOGAF Standard deal with?

The TOGAF standard covers the development of four related types of architecture. These four types of architecture are commonly accepted as subsets of an overall Enterprise Architecture. They are shown in Table 3.

Table 3: Architecture Types Supported by the TOGAF Standard

Architecture Type	Description
Business Architecture	The business strategy, governance, organization, and key business processes.
Data Architecture[3]	The structure of an organization's logical and physical data assets and data management resources.
Application Architecture	A blueprint for the individual applications to be deployed, their interactions, and their relationships to the core business processes of the organization.
Technology Architecture	The logical software and hardware capabilities that are required to support the deployment of business, data, and application services. This includes IT infrastructure, middleware, networks, communications, processing, and standards.

1.5 What does the TOGAF Standard Contain?

The contents of the TOGAF standard reflect the structure and content of an Architecture Capability within an enterprise, as shown in Figure 1.

---

3 Data Architecture is called Information Architecture in some organizations.

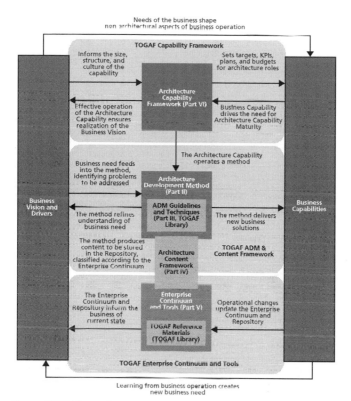

Figure 1: TOGAF Content Overview

Central to the TOGAF framework is the Architecture Development Method (documented in Part II of the standard). The Architecture Capability (documented in Part VI of the standard) operates the method. The method is supported by a number of guidelines and techniques (documented in Part III of the standard, and the TOGAF Library). This produces content to be stored in the repository (documented in

Part IV of the standard), which is classified according to the Enterprise
Continuum (documented in Part V of the standard). The repository can
be initially populated with the TOGAF Reference Models and other
reference materials (documented in the TOGAF Library).

1.5.1 The Architecture Development Method (ADM)

The **ADM** describes how to derive an organization-specific Enterprise
Architecture that addresses business requirements. The ADM is the
major component of the TOGAF framework and provides guidance for
architects on a number of levels:

- It provides a number of **architecture development phases** (Business
  Architecture, Information Systems Architectures, Technology
  Architecture) in a cycle, as an overall process template for architecture
  development activity
- It provides a **narrative of each architecture phase**, describing the
  phase in terms of objectives, approach, inputs, steps, and outputs; the
  inputs and outputs sections provide a definition of the architecture
  content structure and deliverables (a detailed description of the
  phase inputs and phase outputs is given in the Architecture Content
  Framework)
- It provides cross-phase summaries that cover requirements
  management

The ADM is described further in Chapter 2.

1.5.2 ADM Guidelines and Techniques

ADM Guidelines and Techniques provides a number of guidelines
and techniques to support the application of the ADM. The guidelines
include adapting the ADM to deal with a number of usage scenarios,
including different process styles – the use of iteration, and applying
the ADM across the Architecture Landscape. There is also a high-
level description of how to use the TOGAF framework with different
architectural styles using SOA as an example. The techniques support
specific tasks within the ADM (such as capability-based planning,

defining principles, gap analysis, migration planning, risk management, stakeholder management, etc.). Additional guidelines and techniques are also available in the TOGAF Library (for example, guidance on the business scenarios technique).

ADM Guidelines are described further in Chapter 4. ADM Techniques are described in detail in Chapter 3, together with key deliverables.

1.5.3 Architecture Content Framework

The **Architecture Content Framework** provides a detailed model of architectural work products, including deliverables, artifacts within deliverables, and the Architecture Building Blocks (ABBs) that artifacts represent.

The Architecture Content Framework is described further in Chapter 5.

1.5.4 The Enterprise Continuum

The **Enterprise Continuum** provides a model for structuring a virtual repository and provides methods for classifying architecture and solution artifacts, showing how the different types of artifacts evolve, and how they can be leveraged and re-used. This is based on architectures and solutions (models, patterns, architecture descriptions, etc.) that exist within the enterprise and in the industry at large, and which the enterprise has collected for use in the development of its architectures

The Enterprise Continuum is described further in Chapter 6.

1.5.5 The Architecture Capability Framework

The **Architecture Capability Framework** is a set of resources, guidelines, templates, background information, etc. provided to help the architect establish an architecture practice within an organization.

The Architecture Capability Framework is described further in Chapter 7.

Chapter 2
The Architecture
Development Method

This chapter describes the Architecture Development Method (ADM), its relationship to the rest of the TOGAF framework, and high-level considerations for its use. It also includes a summary of each phase within the ADM.

Topics addressed in this chapter include:
- An introduction to the ADM
- The phases of the ADM
- The objectives, steps, inputs, and outputs of the ADM phases
- Requirements Management during the ADM cycle
- Scoping the architecture activity

2.1 What is the ADM?

The ADM, a result of contributions from many architecture practitioners, forms the core of the TOGAF standard. It is a method for deriving organization-specific Enterprise Architectures and is specifically designed to address business requirements. The ADM describes:
- A reliable, proven way of developing and using an Enterprise Architecture
- A method of developing architectures on different levels[4] (business, application, data, technology) that enable the architect to ensure that a complex set of requirements are adequately addressed
- A set of guidelines and techniques for architecture development

---

4 In TOGAF terminology this is termed as a set of architecture domains.

2.2 What are the Phases of the ADM?

The ADM consists of a number of phases that cycle through a range of architecture domains that enable the architect to ensure that a complex set of requirements is adequately addressed. The basic structure of the ADM is shown in Figure 2.

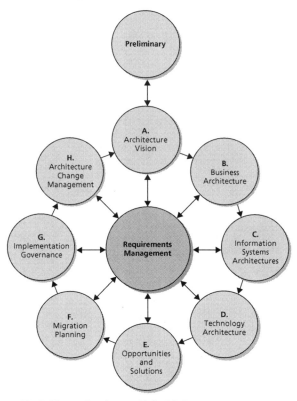

Figure 2: The Architecture Development Method Cycle

The ADM is applied iteratively throughout the entire process, between phases, and within them. Throughout the ADM cycle, there should be frequent validation of results against the original requirements, both those for the whole ADM cycle, and those for the particular phase of the process. Such validation should reconsider scope, detail, schedules, and milestones. Each phase should consider assets produced from previous iterations of the process and external assets from the marketplace, such as other frameworks or models.

The ADM supports the concept of iteration at three levels:

- **Cycling around the ADM**: the ADM is presented in a circular manner indicating that the completion of one phase of architecture work directly feeds into subsequent phases of architecture work
- **Iterating between phases**: the TOGAF standard describes the concept of iterating across phases (e.g., returning to Business Architecture on completion of Technology Architecture)
- **Cycling around a single phase**: the ADM supports repeated execution of the activities within a single ADM phase as a technique for elaborating architectural content

Further information on iteration is given in Part III of the standard (see Chapter 4).

Table 4: Architecture Development Method Activities by Phase

ADM Phase	Activity
Preliminary Phase	Prepare the organization for successful TOGAF architecture projects. Undertake the preparation and initiation activities required to create an Architecture Capability, including the customization of the TOGAF framework, selection of tools, and the definition of Architecture Principles.

ADM Phase	Activity
Requirements Management	Every stage of a TOGAF project is based on and validates business requirements. Requirements are identified, stored, and fed into and out of the relevant ADM phases, which dispose of, address, and prioritize requirements.
Phase A: Architecture Vision	Set the scope, constraints, and expectations for a TOGAF project. Create the Architecture Vision. Identify stakeholders. Validate the business context and create the Statement of Architecture Work. Obtain approvals.
Phase B: Business Architecture Phase C: Information Systems Architectures (Application & Data) Phase D: Technology Architecture	Develop architectures in four domains: 1. Business 2. Information Systems – Application 3. Information Systems – Data 4. Technology In each case, develop the Baseline and Target Architecture and analyze gaps.
Phase E: Opportunities and Solutions	Perform initial implementation planning and the identification of delivery vehicles for the building blocks identified in the previous phases. Determine whether an incremental approach is required, and if so identify Transition Architectures.
Phase F: Migration Planning	Develop detailed Implementation and Migration Plan that addresses how to move from the Baseline to the Target Architecture.
Phase G: Implementation Governance	Provide architectural oversight for the implementation. Prepare and issue Architecture Contracts. Ensure that the implementation project conforms to the architecture.
Phase H: Architecture Change Management	Provide continual monitoring and a change management process to ensure that the architecture responds to the needs of the enterprise and maximizes the value of the architecture to the business.

2.3 The ADM in Detail

The following tables summarize the objectives, steps, and the inputs and outputs[5] of each phase of the ADM cycle.

2.3.1 Preliminary Phase

The Preliminary Phase prepares an organization to undertake successful Enterprise Architecture projects.

An overview of the phase is given below:

Objectives	Steps
Determine the Architecture Capability desired by the organization: • Review the organizational context for conducting Enterprise Architecture • Identify and scope the elements of the enterprise organizations affected by the Architecture Capability • Identify the established frameworks, methods, and processes that intersect with the Architecture Capability • Establish Capability Maturity target Establish the Architecture Capability: • Define and establish the Organizational Model for Enterprise Architecture • Define and establish the detailed process and resources for Architecture Governance • Select and implement tools that support the Architecture Capability • Define the Architecture Principles	Scope the enterprise organizations impacted Confirm governance and support frameworks Define and establish the Enterprise Architecture team and organization Identify and establish Architecture Principles Tailor the TOGAF framework and, if any, other selected architecture frameworks Develop strategy and implementation plans for tools and techniques

---

5 Version numbers for specific deliverables have been omitted from this Pocket Guide since the TOGAF standard states that the ADM numbering scheme is an example and that it should be adapted as appropriate.

Inputs	Outputs
The TOGAF Library	Organizational Model for
Other architecture framework(s)	Enterprise Architecture
Board strategies, business plans, business	Tailored Architecture
strategy, IT Strategy, business principles,	Framework, including
business goals, and business drivers	Architecture Principles
Major frameworks operating in the business	Initial Architecture Repository
Governance and legal frameworks	Restatement of, or reference to,
Architecture Capability	business principles, business
Partnership and contract agreements	goals, and business drivers
Existing organizational model for Enterprise	Request for Architecture Work
Architecture	Architecture Governance
Existing architecture framework, if any,	Framework
including:	
• Architecture method	
• Architecture content	
• Configured and deployed tools	
• Architecture Principles	
• Architecture Repository	

2.3.2 Phase A: Architecture Vision

Phase A is about project establishment and initiates an iteration of the architecture development cycle, setting the scope, constraints, and expectations for the iteration. It is required in order to validate the business context and to create the approved Statement of Architecture Work.

Objectives	Steps
Develop a high-level aspirational vision of the capabilities and business value to be delivered as a result of the proposed Enterprise Architecture	Establish the architecture project
	Identify stakeholders, concerns, and business requirements
	Confirm and elaborate business goals, business drivers, and constraints
Obtain approval for a Statement of Architecture Work that defines a program of works to develop and deploy the architecture outlined in the Architecture Vision	Evaluate capabilities
	Assess readiness for business transformation
	Define scope

Objectives	Steps
	Confirm and elaborate Architecture Principles, including business principles
	Develop Architecture Vision
	Define the Target Architecture value propositions and KPIs
	Identify the business transformation risks and mitigation activities
	Develop Statement of Architecture Work; secure approval

Inputs	Outputs
Request for Architecture Work	Approved Statement of Architecture Work
Business principles, business goals, and business drivers	Refined statements of business principles, business goals, and business drivers
Organization Model for Enterprise Architecture	Architecture Principles
	Capability assessment
Tailored Architecture Framework, including tailored architecture method, architecture content, Architecture Principles, configured and deployed tools	Tailored Architecture Framework
	Architecture Vision, including:
	• Refined key high-level stakeholder requirements
Populated Architecture Repository; that is, existing architecture documentation (framework description, architecture descriptions, existing baseline descriptions, etc.)	Draft Architecture Definition Document, including (when in scope):
	• Baseline Business Architecture (high level)
	• Baseline Data Architecture (high-level)
	• Baseline Application Architecture (high-level)
	• Baseline Technology Architecture (high-level)
	• Target Business Architecture (high-level)
	• Target Data Architecture (high-level)
	• Target Application Architecture (high-level)
	• Target Technology Architecture (high-level)
	Communications Plan
	Additional content populating the Architecture Repository

2.3.3 Phase B: Business Architecture

Phase B is about development of Business Architecture; a holistic representation of business capabilities, end-to-end value delivery, information, and organizational structure, along with the relationships to strategies, products, policies, initiatives, and stakeholders.

Objectives	Steps
Develop the Target Business Architecture that describes how the enterprise needs to operate to achieve the business goals, and respond to the strategic drivers set out in the Architecture Vision in a way that addresses the Statement of Architecture Work and stakeholder concerns	Select reference models, viewpoints, and tools
	Develop Baseline Business Architecture Description
	Develop Target Business Architecture Description
	Perform gap analysis
	Define candidate roadmap components
Identify candidate Architecture Roadmap components based upon gaps between the Baseline and Target Business Architectures	Resolve impacts across the Architecture Landscape
	Conduct formal stakeholder review
	Finalize the Business Architecture
	Create Architecture Definition Document
Inputs	**Outputs**
Request for Architecture Work	Statement of Architecture Work, updated if necessary
Business principles, business goals, and business drivers	Validated business principles, business goals, and business drivers
Capability Assessment	Refined and updated Architecture Principles, if applicable
Communications Plan	
Organization Model for Enterprise Architecture	Draft Architecture Definition Document containing content updates:
Tailored Architecture Framework	• Baseline Business Architecture (detailed), if appropriate
Approved Statement of Architecture Work	
Architecture Principles, including business principles, when pre-existing	• Target Business Architecture (detailed with Business Capabilities, Value Streams, and Organization Map as core artifacts)
Enterprise Continuum	
Architecture Repository	

Inputs	Outputs
Architecture Vision, including: • Refined key high-level stakeholder requirements Draft Architecture Definition Document, including: • Baseline Business Architecture (high-level) • Baseline Data Architecture (high-level) • Baseline Application Architecture (high-level) • Baseline Technology Architecture (high-level) • Target Business Architecture (high-level) • Target Data Architecture (high-level) • Target Application Architecture (high-level) • Target Technology Architecture (high-level)	• Views corresponding to selected viewpoints addressing key stakeholder concerns Draft Architecture Requirements Specification including content updates: • Gap analysis results • Technical requirements • Updated business requirements Business Architecture components of an Architecture Roadmap

2.3.4 Phase C: Information Systems Architectures

Phase C is about documenting the fundamental organization of an organization's IT systems, embodied in the major types of information and the application systems that process them. It involves some combination of Data and Application Architecture, which may be developed either sequentially or concurrently.

2.3.4.1 Data Architecture

Objectives	Steps
Develop the Target Data Architecture that enables the Business Architecture and the Architecture Vision, in a way that addresses the Statement of Architecture Work and stakeholder concerns	Select reference models, viewpoints, and tools
	Develop Baseline Data Architecture Description
	Develop Target Data Architecture Description
	Perform gap analysis
Identify candidate Architecture Roadmap components based upon gaps between the Baseline and Target Data Architectures	Define candidate roadmap components
	Resolve impacts across the Architecture Landscape
	Conduct formal stakeholder review
	Finalize the Data Architecture
	Create Architecture Definition Document

Inputs	Outputs
Request for Architecture Work	Statement of Architecture Work, updated if necessary
Capability Assessment	Validated data principles, or new data principles
Communications Plan	Draft Architecture Definition Document, containing content updates:
Organizational Model for Enterprise Architecture	• Baseline Data Architecture
Tailored Architecture Framework	• Target Data Architecture
Data principles	• Data Architecture views corresponding to the selected viewpoints, addressing key stakeholder concerns
Statement of Architecture Work	Draft Architecture Requirements Specification, including content updates:
Architecture Vision	• Gap analysis results
Architecture Repository	• Data interoperability requirements
Draft Architecture Definition Document, containing:	• Relevant technical requirements that will apply to this evolution of the architecture development cycle
• Baseline Business Architecture (detailed)	• Constraints on the Technology Architecture
• Target Business Architecture (detailed)	• Updated business requirements
• Baseline Data Architecture (high-level)	• Updated application requirements
• Target Data Architecture (high-level)	

Inputs	Outputs
• Baseline Application Architecture (detailed or vision) • Target Application Architecture (detailed or vision) • Baseline Technology Architecture (high-level) • Target Technology Architecture (high-level) Draft Architecture Requirements Specification, including: • Gap analysis results • Relevant technical requirements Business Architecture components of an Architecture Roadmap	Data Architecture components of an Architecture Roadmap

2.3.4.2 Application Architecture

Objectives	Steps
Develop the Target Application Architecture that enables the Business Architecture and the Architecture Vision, in a way that addresses the Statement of Architecture Work and stakeholder concerns Identify candidate Architecture Roadmap components based upon gaps between the Baseline and Target Application Architectures	Select reference models, viewpoints, and tools Develop Baseline Application Architecture Description Develop Target Application Architecture Description Perform gap analysis Define candidate roadmap components Resolve impacts across the Architecture Landscape Conduct formal stakeholder review Finalize the Application Architecture Create Architecture Definition Document
Inputs	**Outputs**
Request for Architecture Work Capability Assessment Communications Plan Organization Model for Enterprise Architecture	Statement of Architecture Work, updated if necessary Validated application principles, or new application principles

Inputs	Outputs
Tailored Architecture Framework	Draft Architecture Definition Document,
Application Principles	containing content updates:
Statement of Architecture Work	• Baseline Application Architecture
Architecture Vision	• Target Application Architecture
Architecture Repository	• Application Architecture views
Draft Architecture Definition	corresponding to the selected
Document, containing:	viewpoints, addressing key stakeholder
• Baseline Business Architecture	concerns
(detailed)	Draft Architecture Requirements
• Target Business Architecture	Specification, including content
(detailed)	updates:
• Baseline Data Architecture	• Gap analysis results
(detailed or high-level)	• Application interoperability
• Target Data Architecture	requirements
(detailed or high-level)	• Relevant technical requirements that
• Baseline Application Architecture	will apply to this evolution of the
(high-level)	architecture development cycle
• Target Application Architecture	• Constraints on the Technology
(high-level)	Architecture
• Baseline Technology Architecture	• Updated business requirements
(high-level)	• Updated data requirements
• Target Technology Architecture	Application Architecture components of
(high-level)	an Architecture Roadmap
Draft Architecture Requirements	
Specification, including:	
• Gap analysis results	
• Relevant technical requirements	
Business and Data Architecture	
components of an Architecture	
Roadmap	

2.3.5 Phase D: Technology Architecture

Phase D is about documenting the fundamental organization of the
IT systems, embodied in the hardware, software, and communications
technology.

Objectives	Steps
Develop the Target Technology Architecture that enables the Architecture Vision, target business, data, and application building blocks to be delivered through technology components and technology services, in a way that addresses the Statement of Architecture Work and stakeholder concerns	Select reference models, viewpoints, and tools
	Develop Baseline Technology Architecture Description
	Develop Target Technology Architecture Description
	Perform gap analysis
	Define candidate roadmap components
	Resolve impacts across the Architecture Landscape
	Conduct formal stakeholder review
Identify candidate Architecture Roadmap components based upon gaps between the Baseline and Target Technology Architectures	Finalize the Technology Architecture
	Create Architecture Definition Document

Inputs	Outputs
Request for Architecture Work	Statement of Architecture Work, updated if necessary
Capability Assessment	Validated technology principles or new technology principles (if generated here)
Communications Plan	
Organization Model for Enterprise Architecture	Draft Architecture Definition Document, containing content updates.
Tailored Architecture Framework	
Technology principles	• Baseline Technology Architecture, if appropriate
Statement of Architecture Work	• Target Technology Architecture
Architecture Vision	• Technology Architecture views corresponding to the selected viewpoints, addressing key stakeholder concerns
Architecture Repository	
Draft Architecture Definition Document, containing:	
• Baseline Business Architecture (detailed)	Draft Architecture Requirements Specification, including content updates:
• Target Business Architecture (detailed)	• Gap analysis report
• Baseline Data Architecture (detailed)	• Requirements output from Phases B and C
• Target Data Architecture (detailed)	• Updated technology requirements
• Baseline Application Architecture (detailed)	Technology Architecture components of an Architecture Roadmap
• Target Application Architecture (detailed)	

Inputs	Outputs
• Baseline Technology Architecture (high-level) • Target Technology Architecture (high-level) Draft Architecture Requirements Specification, including: • Gap analysis results • Relevant technical requirements Business, Data, and Application Architecture components of an Architecture Roadmap	

2.3.6 Phase E: Opportunities and Solutions

Phase E is the first phase which is directly concerned with implementation. It describes the process of identifying delivery vehicles (projects, programs, or portfolios) that deliver the Target Architecture identified in previous phases.

Objectives	Steps
Generate the initial complete version of the Architecture Roadmap, based upon the gap analysis and candidate Architecture Roadmap components from Phases B, C, and D Determine whether an incremental approach is required, and if so identify Transition Architectures that will deliver continuous business value Define the overall Solution Building Blocks (SBBs) to finalize the Target Architecture based on the Architecture Building Blocks (ABBs)	Determine/confirm key corporate change attributes Determine business constraints for implementation Review and consolidate gap analysis results from Phases B to D Review consolidated requirements across related business functions Consolidate and reconcile interoperability requirements Refine and validate dependencies Confirm readiness and risk for business transformation Formulate Implementation and Migration Strategy Identify and group major work packages

Objectives	Steps
	Identify Transition Architectures
	Create Architecture Roadmap & Implementation and Migration Plan

Inputs	Outputs
Product Information	Statement of Architecture Work, updated if necessary
Request for Architecture Work	Architecture Vision, updated if necessary
Capability Assessment	Draft Architecture Definition
Communications Plan	Document, including:
Planning Methodologies	• Transition Architectures, number and scope, if any
Organizational Model for Enterprise Architecture	Draft Architecture Requirements Specification
Governance Models and Frameworks	Capability Assessment, including:
Tailored Architecture Framework	• Business Capability
Statement of Architecture Work	• IT Capability
Architecture Vision	Architecture Roadmap, including:
Architecture Repository	• Work package portfolio
Draft Architecture Definition Document	• Identification of Transition Architectures, if any
Draft Architecture Requirements Specification	• Implementation recommendations
Change Requests for existing programs and projects	Implementation and Migration Plan (outline), including:
Candidate Architecture Roadmap components from Phases B, C, and D	• Implementation and Migration Strategy

2.3.7 Phase F: Migration Planning

Phase F addresses migration planning; that is, how to move from the Baseline to the Target Architectures by finalizing a detailed Implementation and Migration Plan.

Objectives	Steps
Finalize the Architecture Roadmap and the supporting Implementation and Migration Plan Ensure that the Implementation and Migration Plan is coordinated with the enterprise's approach to managing and implementing change in the enterprise's overall change portfolio Ensure that the business value and cost of work packages and Transition Architectures is understood by key stakeholders	Confirm management framework interactions for the Implementation and Migration Plan Assign a business value to each work package Estimate resource requirements, project timings, and availability/delivery vehicle Prioritize the migration projects through the conduct of a cost/benefit assessment and risk validation Confirm Architecture Roadmap and update Architecture Definition Document Complete the Implementation and Migration Plan Complete the architecture development cycle and document lessons learned
Inputs	**Outputs**
Request for Architecture Work Communications Plan Organization Model for Enterprise Architecture Governance Models and Frameworks Tailored Architecture Framework Statement of Architecture Work Architecture Vision Architecture Repository Draft Architecture Definition Document, including: • Transition Architectures, if any Draft Architecture Requirements Specification Change Requests for existing programs and projects Architecture Roadmap	Implementation and Migration Plan (detailed), including: • Implementation and Migration Strategy • Project and portfolio breakdown of the implementation • Project charters (optional) Finalized Architecture Definition Document, including: • Finalized Transition Architectures, if any Finalized Architecture Requirements Specification Finalized Architecture Roadmap Re-usable Architecture Building Blocks Requests for Architecture Work for a new iteration of the ADM cycle (if any)

Inputs	Outputs
Capability Assessment, including: • Business Capability • IT Capability Implementation and Migration Plan (outline), including: • High-level Implementation and Migration Strategy	Implementation Governance Model Change Requests for the Architecture Capability arising from lessons learned

2.3.8 Phase G: Implementation Governance

Phase G defines how the architecture constrains the implementation projects, monitors it while building it, and produces a signed Architecture Contract.

Objectives	Steps
Ensure conformance with the Target Architecture by implementation projects Perform appropriate Architecture Governance functions for the solution and any implementation-driven architecture Change Requests	Confirm scope and priorities for deployment with development management Identify deployment resources and skills Guide development of solutions deployment Perform Enterprise Architecture compliance reviews Implement business and IT operations Perform post-implementation review and close the implementation
Inputs	**Outputs**
Request for Architecture Work Capability Assessment Organization Model for Enterprise Architecture Tailored Architecture Framework Statement of Architecture Work Architecture Vision Architecture Repository Architecture Definition Document Architecture Requirements Specification	Architecture Contract (signed) Compliance Assessments Change Requests Architecture-compliant solutions deployed, including: • The architecture-compliant implemented system • Populated Architecture Repository • Architecture compliance recommendations and dispensations

Inputs	Outputs

Architecture Roadmap
Implementation Governance
   Model
Architecture Contract
Request for Architecture Work
   identified in Phases E and F
Implementation and Migration
   Plan
	• Recommendations on service delivery
	  requirements
	• Recommendations on performance
	  metrics
	• Service Level Agreements (SLAs)
	• Architecture Vision, updated post-
	  implementation
	• Architecture Definition Document,
	  updated post-implementation
	• Business and IT operating models for
	  the implemented solution

2.3.9 Phase H: Architecture Change Management

Phase H ensures that changes to the architecture are managed in a controlled manner.

Objectives	Steps

Ensure that the architecture lifecycle
  is maintained
Ensure that the Architecture
  Governance Framework is
  executed
Ensure that the Enterprise
  Architecture Capability meets
  current requirements
	Establish value realization process
	Deploy monitoring tools
	Manage risks
	Provide analysis for architecture change
	  management
	Develop change requirements to meet
	  performance targets
	Manage governance process
	Activate the process to implement
	  change

Inputs	**Outputs**

Request for Architecture Work
Organization Model for Enterprise
  Architecture
Tailored Architecture Framework
Statement of Architecture Work
Architecture Vision
Architecture Repository
Architecture Definition Document
	Architecture updates
	Changes to architecture framework and
	  principles
	New Request for Architecture Work, to
	  initiate another cycle of the ADM
	Statement of Architecture Work,
	  updated if necessary

Inputs	Outputs
Architecture Requirements Specification	Architecture Contract, updated if necessary
Architecture Roadmap	Compliance Assessments, updated if necessary
Change Requests due to technology changes	
Change Requests due to business changes	
Change Requests from lessons learned	
Implementation Governance Model	
Architecture Contract (signed)	
Compliance Assessments	
Implementation and Migration Plan	

2.3.10 Requirements Management

The process of managing architecture requirements applies to all phases of the ADM cycle. The Requirements Management process is a dynamic process, which addresses the identification of requirements for the enterprise, storing them, and then feeding them in and out of the relevant ADM phases. As shown in Figure 2, this process is central to driving the ADM process.

The ability to deal with changes in the requirements is crucial to the ADM process, since architecture by its very nature deals with uncertainty and change, bridging the divide between the aspirations of the stakeholders and what can be delivered as a practical solution.

Objectives	Steps
Ensure that the Requirements Management process is sustained and operates for all relevant ADM phases Manage architecture requirements identified during any execution of the ADM cycle or a phase Ensure that relevant architecture requirements are available for use by each phase as the phase is executed	Identify/document requirements Baseline requirements Monitor baseline requirements Identify changed requirements; remove, add, modify, and re-assess priorities Identify changed requirements and record priorities; identify and resolve conflicts; generate requirements impact statements Assess impact of changed requirements on current and previous ADM phases Implement requirements arising from Phase H Update the Architecture Requirements Repository Implement change in the current phase Assess and revise gap analysis for past phases
Inputs	**Outputs**
The inputs to the Requirements Management process are the requirements-related outputs from each ADM phase. The first high-level requirements are produced as part of the Architecture Vision. Each architecture domain then generates detailed requirements. Deliverables in later ADM phases contain mappings to new types of requirements (for example, conformance requirements).	Changed requirements Requirements Impact Assessment, which identifies the phases of the ADM that need to be revisited to address any changes. The final version must include the full implications of the requirements (e.g., costs, timescales, and business metrics).

2.4 Scoping the Architecture Activity

The ADM defines a recommended sequence for the various phases and steps involved in developing an organization-wide Enterprise Architecture, but the ADM cannot determine scope: this must be determined by the organization itself.

There are many reasons to constrain (or restrict) the scope of the architectural activity to be undertaken, most of which relate to limits in:

- The organizational authority of the team producing the architecture
- The objectives and stakeholder concerns to be addressed within the architecture
- The availability of people, finance, and other resources

The scope chosen for the architecture activity should ideally allow the work of all architects within the enterprise to be effectively governed and integrated. This requires a set of aligned "architecture partitions" that ensure architects are not working on duplicate or conflicting activities. It also requires the definition of re-use and compliance relationships between architecture partitions. The division of the enterprise and its architecture-related activity is addressed in Part III of the standard (see Chapter 4).

Table 5 shows the four dimensions in which the scope may be defined and limited.

Table 5: Dimensions for Limiting the Scope of the Architecture Activity

Dimension	Considerations
Breadth	What is the full extent of the enterprise, and what part of that extent should the architecting effort deal with? Many enterprises are very large, effectively comprising a federation of organizational units that could be considered enterprises in their own right. The modern enterprise increasingly extends beyond its traditional boundaries, to embrace a fuzzy combination of traditional business enterprise combined with suppliers, customers, and partners.
Depth	To what level of detail should the architecting effort go? How much architecture is "enough"? What is the appropriate demarcation between the architecture effort and other, related activities (system design, system engineering, system development)?

Dimension	Considerations
Time Period	What is the time period that needs to be articulated for the Architecture Vision, and does it make sense (in terms of practicality and resources) for the same period to be covered in the detailed architecture description? If not, how many Transition Architectures are to be defined, and what are their time periods?
Architecture Domains	A complete Enterprise Architecture description should contain all four architecture domains (Business, Data, Application, Technology), but the realities of resource and time constraints often mean there is not enough time, funding, or resources to build a top-down, all-inclusive architecture description encompassing all four architecture domains, even if the enterprise scope is chosen to be less than the full extent of the overall enterprise.

Chapter 3
Key Techniques and Deliverables of the ADM Cycle

This chapter will help you to understand the key techniques and deliverables of the ADM cycle. Table 6 gives a roadmap to this chapter by the ADM phase in which the techniques and deliverables are used. For each point, key facts are presented.

Table 6: Roadmap to Chapter 3

ADM Phase	Reference(s)
Preliminary Phase	Section 3.1, Tailored Architecture Framework
	Section 3.2, Organizational Model for Enterprise Architecture
	Section 3.3, Architecture Principles
	Section 3.4, Business Principles, Business Goals, and Business Drivers
	Section 3.5, Architecture Repository
	Section 3.6, Architecture Tools & Techniques
	Section 3.7, Request for Architecture Work
Phase A: Architecture Vision	Section 3.8, Statement of Architecture Work
	Section 3.9, Architecture Vision
	Section 3.10, Stakeholder Management
	Section 3.11, Communications Plan
	Section 3.12, Business Transformation Readiness Assessment
	Section 3.13, Capability Assessment
	Section 3.14, Risk Management
	Section 3.15, Architecture Definition Document
	Section 3.20, Architecture Viewpoints
	Section 3.21, Architecture Views

ADM Phase	Reference(s)
Phase B: Business Architecture	Section 3.14, Risk Management Section 3.15, Architecture Definition Document Section 3.16, Architecture Requirements Specification Section 3.17, Architecture Roadmap Section 3.18, Business Scenarios Section 3.19, Gap Analysis Section 3.20, Architecture Viewpoints Section 3.21, Architecture Views Section 3.22, Architecture Building Blocks Section 3.23, Solution Building Blocks
Phase C: Information Systems Architectures	Section 3.15, Architecture Definition Document Section 3.16, Architecture Requirements Specification Section 3.17, Architecture Roadmap Section 3.19, Gap Analysis Section 3.20, Architecture Viewpoints Section 3.21, Architecture Views Section 3.22, Architecture Building Blocks Section 3.23, Solution Building Blocks
Phase D: Technology Architecture	Section 3.15, Architecture Definition Document Section 3.16, Architecture Requirements Specification Section 3.17, Architecture Roadmap Section 3.19, Gap Analysis Section 3.20, Architecture Viewpoints Section 3.21, Architecture Views Section 3.22, Architecture Building Blocks Section 3.23, Solution Building Blocks
Phase E: Opportunities and Solutions	Section 3.15, Architecture Definition Document Section 3.19, Gap Analysis Section 3.22, Architecture Building Blocks Section 3.23, Solution Building Blocks Section 3.24, Capability-Based Planning Section 3.25, Migration Planning Techniques Section 3.26, Implementation and Migration Plan Section 3.27, Transition Architecture Section 3.28, Implementation Governance Model

ADM Phase	Reference(s)
Phase F: Migration Planning	Section 3.24, Capability-Based Planning Section 3.25, Migration Planning Techniques Section 3.26, Implementation and Migration Plan Section 3.27, Transition Architecture Section 3.28, Implementation Governance Model
Phase G: Implementation Governance	Section 3.28, Implementation Governance Model Section 3.29, Architecture Contracts Section 3.30, Change Request Section 3.31, Compliance Assessment
Phase H: Architecture Change Management	Section 3.28, Implementation Governance Model Section 3.29, Architecture Contracts Section 3.31, Compliance Assessment Section 3.32, Requirements Impact Assessment
ADM Architecture Requirements Management	Section 3.16, Architecture Requirements Specification Section 3.32, Requirements Impact Assessment

3.1 Tailored Architecture Framework

Selecting and tailoring a framework is the practical starting point for an architecture project. Building on the TOGAF standard has a number of advantages over creating a framework from scratch:

- It avoids the initial panic when the scale of the task becomes apparent
- Its use is systematic – "codified common sense"
- It captures what others have found to work in real life
- It has a baseline set of resources to re-use
- The TOGAF Library defines reference material that can be used to populate the Enterprise Continuum

However, before the TOGAF framework can be effectively used within an architecture project, tailoring at a number of levels is necessary and should occur in the Preliminary Phase.

Firstly, it is necessary to tailor the TOGAF model for integration into the enterprise. This tailoring will include integration with management frameworks, customization of terminology, development

of presentational styles, selection, configuration, and deployment of
architecture tools, etc. The formality and detail of any frameworks
adopted should also align with other contextual factors for the enterprise,
such as culture, stakeholders, commercial models for Enterprise
Architecture, and the existing level of Architecture Capability.

Once the framework has been tailored to the enterprise, further tailoring
is necessary in order to tailor the framework for the specific architecture
project. Tailoring at this level will select appropriate deliverables and
artifacts to meet project and stakeholder needs.

The following contents are typical within a Tailored Architecture
Framework:
- Tailored architecture method
- Tailored architecture content (deliverables and artifacts)
- Configured and deployed tools
- Interfaces with governance models and other frameworks:
  - Corporate Business Planning
  - Enterprise Architecture
  - Portfolio, Program, Project Management
  - System Development/Engineering
  - Operations (Services)

3.2 Organizational Model for Enterprise Architecture

An important deliverable produced in the Preliminary Phase is the
Organizational Model for Enterprise Architecture.

In order for an architecture framework to be used successfully, it must
be supported by the correct organization, roles, and responsibilities
within the enterprise. Of particular importance is the definition of
boundaries between different Enterprise Architecture practitioners and
the governance relationships that span across these boundaries.

Typical contents of an Organizational Model for Enterprise Architecture are:

- Scope of organizations impacted
- Maturity assessment, gaps, and resolution approach
- Roles and responsibilities for architecture team(s)
- Constraints on architecture work
- Budget requirements
- Governance and support strategy

3.3 Architecture Principles

This set of documentation is an initial output of the Preliminary Phase. It is the set of general rules and guidelines for the architecture being developed. See Part III of the standard (Architecture Principles) for guidelines and a detailed set of generic Architecture Principles. The suggested contents of this document are business principles, data principles, application principles, and technology principles.

3.3.1 Developing Architecture Principles

Architecture Principles are typically developed by the Enterprise Architects, in conjunction with the key stakeholders, and are approved by the Architecture Board.

The following typically influences the development of Architecture Principles:

- **Enterprise mission and plans** – the mission, plans, and organizational infrastructure of the enterprise
- **Enterprise strategic initiatives** – the characteristics of the enterprise – its strengths, weaknesses, opportunities, and threats – and its current enterprise-wide initiatives (such as process improvement and quality management)
- **External constraints** – market factors (time-to-market imperatives, customer expectations, etc.); existing and potential legislation
- **Current systems and technology** – the set of information resources deployed within the enterprise, including systems documentation,

equipment inventories, network configuration diagrams, policies, and
procedures
• **Computer industry trends** – predictions about the usage, availability,
and cost of computer and communication technologies, taken from
credible sources along with associated best practices presently in use

3.3.2 Defining Architecture Principles

Depending on the organization, principles may be established within
different domains and at different levels. Two key domains inform the
development and utilization of architecture:
• **Enterprise principles** provide a basis for decision-making throughout
an enterprise and dictate how the organization fulfills its mission
Such principles are commonly used as a means of harmonizing
decision-making. They are a key element in a successful Architecture
Governance strategy. Within the broad domain of enterprise
principles, it is common to have subsidiary principles within a business
or organizational unit; for example IT, HR, domestic operations, or
overseas operations.
• **Architecture principles** are a set of principles that relate to
architecture work
They reflect consensus across the enterprise, and embody the spirit
of the Enterprise Architecture. Architecture Principles govern the
architecture process, affecting the development, maintenance, and use
of the Enterprise Architecture.

The TOGAF standard includes a recommended template for describing
principles. In addition to a definition statement, each principle should
have associated rationale and implications statements, both to promote
understanding and acceptance of the principles themselves, and to
support the use of the principles in explaining and justifying why specific
decisions are made.

Table 7: TOGAF Template for Defining Principles

Name	Should both represent the essence of the rule as well as be easy to remember. Specific technology platforms should not be mentioned in the name or statement of a principle. Avoid ambiguous words in the name and in the statement such as: "support", "open", "consider", and for lack of good measure the word "avoid", itself, be careful with "manage(ment)", and look for unnecessary adjectives and adverbs (fluff).
Statement	Should succinctly and unambiguously communicate the fundamental rule. For the most part, the principles statements for managing information are similar among organizations. It is vital that the principles statement be unambiguous.
Rationale	Should highlight the business benefits of adhering to the principle, using business terminology. Point to the similarity of information and technology principles to the principles governing business operations. Also describe the relationship to other principles, and the intentions regarding a balanced interpretation. Describe situations where one principle would be given precedence or carry more weight than another for making a decision.
Implications	Should highlight the requirements, both for the business and IT, for carrying out the principle – in terms of resources, costs, and activities/tasks. It will often be apparent that current systems, standards, or practices would be incongruent with the principle upon adoption. The impact on the business and consequences of adopting a principle should be clearly stated. The reader should readily discern the answer to: "How does this affect me?" It is important not to oversimplify, trivialize, or judge the merit of the impact. Some of the implications will be identified as potential impacts only, and may be speculative rather than fully analyzed.

3.3.3 Qualities of Principles

There are five criteria that distinguish a good set of principles, as shown in Table 8.

Table 8: Recommended Criteria for Quality Principles

Criteria	Description
Understandability	The underlying tenets of a principle can be quickly grasped and understood by individuals throughout the organization. The intention of the principle is clear and unambiguous, so that violations, whether intentional or not, are minimized.
Robustness	Principles should enable good quality decisions about architectures and plans to be made, and enforceable policies and standards to be created. Each principle should be sufficiently definitive and precise to support consistent decision-making in complex, potentially controversial situations.
Completeness	Every potentially important principle governing the management of information and technology for the organization is defined. The principles cover every situation perceived.
Consistency	Strict adherence to one principle may require a loose interpretation of another principle. The set of principles must be expressed in a way that allows a balance of interpretations. Principles should not be contradictory to the point where adhering to one principle would violate the spirit of another. Every word in a principle statement should be carefully chosen to allow consistent yet flexible interpretation.
Stability	Principles should be enduring, yet able to accommodate changes. An amendment process should be established for adding, removing, or altering principles after they are ratified initially.

3.3.4 Applying Architecture Principles

Architecture Principles are used to capture the fundamental truths about how the enterprise will use and deploy IT resources and assets. The principles are used in a number of different ways:

1. To provide a framework within which the enterprise can start to make conscious decisions about Enterprise Architecture and projects that implement the target Enterprise Architecture

2. As a guide to establishing relevant evaluation criteria, thus exerting strong influence on the selection of products, solutions, or solution architectures in the later stages of managing compliance to the Enterprise Architecture

3. As drivers for defining the functional requirements of the architecture

4. As an input to assessing both existing implementations and the future strategic portfolio, for compliance with the defined architectures; these assessments will provide valuable insights into the transition activities needed to implement an architecture, in support of business goals and priorities

5. The Rationale statements highlight the value of the architecture to the enterprise, and therefore provide a basis for justifying architecture activities

6. The Implications statements provide an outline of the key tasks, resources, and potential costs to the enterprise of following the principle; they also provide valuable inputs to future transition initiatives and planning activities

7. To support the Architecture Governance activities in terms of:
   – Providing a "back-stop" for the standard Architecture Compliance assessments where some interpretation is allowed or required
   – Supporting a decision to initiate a dispensation request where the implications of a particular architecture amendment cannot be resolved within local operating procedure

Principles are inter-related, and need to be applied as a set. Principles will sometimes compete; for example, the principles of "accessibility" and "security". Each principle must be considered in the context of "all other things being equal". At times a decision will be required as to which principle will take precedence on a particular issue. The rationale for such decisions should always be documented. The fact that a principle seems self-evident does not mean that the principle is actually observed in an organization, even when there are verbal acknowledgements of the principle. Although specific penalties are not prescribed in a declaration of principles, violations of principles generally cause operational problems and inhibit the ability of the organization to fulfill its mission.

3.4 Business Principles, Business Goals, and Business Drivers

A statement of the business principles, goals, and drivers has usually been defined elsewhere in the enterprise prior to the architecture activity. They are restated as an output of the Preliminary Phase and reviewed again as a part of Phase A: Architecture Vision. The activity in Phase A is to ensure that the current definitions are correct and clear. Part III of the standard contains an example set of nine business principles that are a useful starting point.

There is no defined content for this deliverable as its content and structure is likely to vary considerably from one organization to the next.

3.5 Architecture Repository

The Architecture Repository acts as a holding area for all architecture-related projects within the enterprise. The repository allows projects to manage their deliverables, locate re-usable assets, and publish outputs to stakeholders and other interested parties.

See Section 6.3 for a description of the content of an Architecture Repository. The following contents are typical within an Architecture Repository:
- Architecture Framework
- Standards Information Base
- Architecture Landscape
- Reference Library
- Governance Log
- Architecture Requirements
- Solutions Landscape

3.6 Architecture Tools & Techniques

As part of the Preliminary Phase, the architect should develop a strategy and implementation plan for tools and techniques to support the architecture activity. The TOGAF standard does not require or recommend any specific tool; instead it recommends a strategy that reflects the understanding and level of formality required by the stakeholders. The TOGAF standard provides a brief commentary on issues in tools standardization in Part V of the standard, Chapter 38.

3.7 Request for Architecture Work

This is a document that is sent from the sponsoring organization to the architecture organization to trigger the start of an architecture development cycle. It is produced with the assistance of the architecture organization as an output of the Preliminary Phase. Requests for Architecture Work will also be created as a result of approved architecture Change Requests, or terms of reference for architecture work originating from migration planning.

In general, all the information in this document should be at a high level. The suggested contents of this document are as follows:
- Organization sponsors
- Organization's mission statement
- Business goals (and changes)
- Strategic plans of the business
- Time limits
- Changes in the business environment
- Organizational constraints
- Budget information, financial constraints
- External constraints, business constraints
- Current business system description
- Current architecture/IT system description
- Description of developing organization
- Description of resources available to developing organization

3.8 Statement of Architecture Work

The Statement of Architecture Work is created as a deliverable of Phase A, and is effectively a contract between the architecting organization and the sponsor of the architecture project. This document is a response to the Request for Architecture Work input document (see Section 3.6). It should describe an overall plan to address the request for work and propose how solutions to the problems that have been identified will be addressed through the architecture process.

The suggested contents of this document are as follows:
• Title
• Architecture project request and background
• Architecture project description and scope
• Overview of Architecture Vision
• Specific change of scope procedures
• Roles, responsibilities, and deliverables
• Acceptance criteria and procedures
• Architecture project plan and schedule
• Approvals

3.9 Architecture Vision

The Architecture Vision is created in Phase A and provides a high-level summary of the changes to the enterprise that will follow from successful deployment of the Target Architecture. The purpose of the vision is to agree at the outset what the desired outcome should be for the architecture, so that architects can then focus on the detail necessary to validate feasibility. Providing an Architecture Vision also supports stakeholder communication by providing a summary version of the full Architecture Definition.

Business scenarios are an appropriate and important technique that can be used as part of the process in developing an Architecture Vision document.

The suggested contents are as follows:
- Problem description:
  - Stakeholders and their concerns
  - List of issues/scenarios to be addressed
- Objective of the Statement of Architecture Work
- Summary views necessary for the Request for Architecture Work and the high-level Business, Application, Data, and Technology Architectures
- Mapped requirements
- Reference to Draft Architecture Definition Document

3.10 Stakeholder Management

Stakeholder management is an important discipline that successful architects can use to win support from others. It helps them ensure that their projects succeed where others fail. The technique should be used during Phase A to identify the key players in the engagement, and also be updated throughout each phase. The output of this process forms the start of the Communications Plan (see Section 3.11).

The benefits of successful stakeholder management are that:
- The most powerful stakeholders can be identified early and their input can then be used to shape the architecture; this ensures their support and improves the quality of the models produced
- Support from the more powerful stakeholders will help the engagement win more resource[s], thus making the architecture engagement more likely to succeed
- By communicating with stakeholders early and frequently, the architecture team can ensure that they fully understand the architecture process, and the benefits of Enterprise Architecture; this means they can support the architecture team more actively when necessary
- The architecture team can more effectively anticipate likely reactions to the architecture models and reports, and can build into the plan

the actions that will be needed to capitalize on positive reaction whilst avoiding or addressing any negative reactions

- The architecture team can identify conflicting or competing objectives among stakeholders early and develop a strategy to resolve the issues arising from them

3.10.1 Steps in the Stakeholder Management Process
Step 1: Identify Stakeholders
The first task is to determine who the main Enterprise Architecture stakeholders are.

A sample stakeholder analysis that distinguishes 22 types of stakeholder, in five broad categories, is shown in Figure 3.

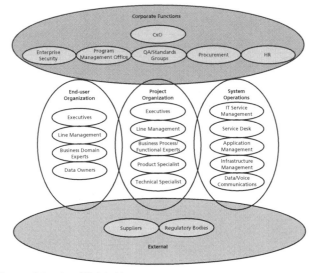

Figure 3: Categories of Stakeholder

Step 2: Classify Stakeholder Positions

Develop a good understanding of the most important stakeholders and record this analysis (as shown in the example in Table 9) for reference and refresh during the project.

Table 9: Example Stakeholder Analysis

Stake-holder Group	Stake-holder	Ability to Disrupt the Change	Current Under-standing	Required Under-standing	Current Commit-ment	Required Commit-ment	Required Support
CIO	John Smith	H	M	H	L	M	H
CFO	Jeff Brown	M	M	M	L	M	M

Step 3: Determine Stakeholder Management Approach

This step enables the team to easily see which stakeholders are expected to be blockers or critics, and which stakeholders are likely to be advocates and supporters of the initiative.

Work out stakeholder power, influence, and interest, so as to focus the Enterprise Architecture engagement on the key individuals. These can be mapped onto a power/interest matrix, which also indicates the strategy you need to adopt for engaging with them.

Figure 4 shows an example power grid matrix.

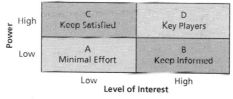

Figure 4: Power Grid

Step 4: Tailor Engagement Deliverables
Identify catalogs, matrices, and diagrams that the architecture
engagement needs to produce and validate with each stakeholder group
to deliver an effective architecture model.

It is important to pay particular attention to stakeholder interests by
defining specific catalogs, matrices, and diagrams that are relevant for a
particular Enterprise Architecture model. This enables the architecture
to be communicated to, and understood by, all the stakeholders, and
enables them to verify that the Enterprise Architecture initiative will
address their concerns.

3.11 Communications Plan

Enterprise Architectures contain large volumes of complex and
inter-dependent information. Effective communication of targeted
information to the right stakeholders at the right time is a critical success
factor for Enterprise Architecture. Development of a Communications
Plan for architecture in Phase A allows for this communication to be
carried out within a planned and managed process.

Typical contents of a Communications Plan are:
• Identification of stakeholders and grouping by communication
  requirements
• Identification of communication needs, key messages in relation to the
  Architecture Vision, communication risks, and Critical Success Factors
  (CSFs)
• Identification of mechanisms that will be used to communicate with
  stakeholders and allow access to architecture information, such as
  meetings, newsletters, repositories, etc.
• Identification of a communications timetable, showing which
  communications will occur with which stakeholder groups at what
  time and in what location

3.12 Business Transformation Readiness Assessment

The technique known as Business Transformation Readiness Assessment is carried out in Phase A and is used for evaluating and quantifying an organization's readiness to undergo change. Understanding the readiness of the organization to accept change, identifying the issues, and then dealing with them is a key part of successful architecture transformation. This assessment is recommended to be a joint effort between corporate staff, lines of business, and IT planners.

The recommended activities are:
- Determine the readiness factors that will impact the organization
- Present the readiness factors using maturity models
- Assess the risks for each readiness factor and identify improvement actions to mitigate the risk
- Document the findings into the Capability Assessment (see Section 3.13), and later incorporate the actions into the Implementation and Migration Plan

3.13 Capability Assessment

Before embarking upon a detailed Architecture Definition, it is valuable to understand the baseline and target capability level of the enterprise. This Capability Assessment is first carried out in Phase A, and updated in Phase E. It can be examined on several levels:
- What is the capability level of the enterprise as a whole? Where does the enterprise wish to increase or optimize capability? What are the architectural focus areas that will support the desired development of the enterprise?
- What is the capability or maturity level of the IT function within the enterprise? What are the likely implications of conducting the architecture project in terms of design governance, operational governance, skills, and organization structure? What is an appropriate style, level of formality, and amount of detail for the architecture project to fit with the culture and capability of the IT organization?

- What is the capability and maturity of the architecture function within the enterprise? What architectural assets are currently in existence? Are they maintained and accurate? What standards and reference models need to be considered? Are there likely to be opportunities to create re-usable assets during the architecture project?
- Where capability gaps exist, to what extent is the business ready to transform in order to reach the target capability? What are the risks to transformation, cultural barriers, and other considerations to be addressed beyond the basic capability gap?

The following contents are typical within a Capability Assessment deliverable:

- Business Capability Assessment, including:
  - Capabilities of the business
  - Baseline state assessment of the performance level of each capability
  - Future state aspiration for the performance level of each capability
  - Baseline state assessment of how each capability is realized
  - Future state aspiration for how each capability should be realized
  - Assessment of likely impacts to the business organization resulting from the successful deployment of the Target Architecture
- IT Capability Assessment, including:
  - Baseline and target maturity level of change process
  - Baseline and target maturity level of operational processes
  - Baseline capability and capacity assessment
  - Assessment of likely impacts to the IT organization resulting from the successful deployment of the Target Architecture
- Architecture Maturity Assessment, including:
  - Architecture Governance processes, organization, roles, and responsibilities
  - Architecture skills assessment
  - Breadth, depth, and quality of landscape definition within the Architecture Repository
  - Breadth, depth, and quality of standards definition within the Architecture Repository

- Breadth, depth, and quality of reference model definition within the
  Architecture Repository
- Assessment of re-use potential
• Business Transformation Readiness Assessment, including:
  - Readiness factors
  - Vision for each readiness factor
  - Current and target readiness ratings
  - Readiness risks

3.14 Risk Management

Identification of business transformation risks and mitigation activities is
first determined in Phase A. Risk management, documented in Part III
of the standard, Chapter 27, is a technique used to mitigate risk when
implementing an architecture project. It includes a process for managing
risk consisting of the following activities:
• Risk classification
• Risk identification
• Initial risk assessment
• Risk mitigation and residual risk assessment
• Risk monitoring

It is recommended that risk mitigation activities be included within the
Statement of Architecture Work.

3.15 Architecture Definition Document

The Architecture Definition Document is the deliverable container for
the core architectural artifacts created during a project and for important
related information. The Architecture Definition Document spans all
architecture domains (Business, Data, Application, and Technology) and
also examines all relevant states of the architecture (baseline, transition,
and target).

It is first created in Phase A, where it is populated with artifacts created
to support the Architecture Vision. It is updated in Phase B, with

Business Architecture-related material, and subsequently updated with Information Systems Architecture material in Phase C, and then with Technology Architecture material in Phase D. Where the scope of change to implement the Target Architecture requires an incremental approach, the Architecture Definition Document will be updated to include one or more Transition Architectures in Phase E (see Section 3.27).

The Architecture Definition Document is a companion to the Architecture Requirements Specification, with a complementary objective:

- The Architecture Definition Document provides a qualitative view of the solution and aims to communicate the intent of the architects
- The Architecture Requirements Specification provides a quantitative view of the solution, stating measurable criteria that must be met during the implementation of the architecture

The following contents are typically found within an Architecture Definition Document:

- Scope
- Goals, objectives, and constraints
- Architecture Principles
- Baseline Architecture
- Architecture models (for each state to be modeled):
  - Business Architecture models
  - Data Architecture models
  - Application Architecture models
  - Technology Architecture models
- Rationale and justification for architectural approach
- Mapping to Architecture Repository:
  - Mapping to Architecture Landscape
  - Mapping to reference models
  - Mapping to standards
  - Re-use assessment

- Gap analysis
- Impact assessment
- Transition Architecture (see Section 3.27)

The following sections look at each of the architectures in more detail.

3.15.1 Business Architecture

The Business Architecture is developed in Phase B. The topics that should be addressed in the Architecture Definition Document related to Business Architecture are as follows:

- Baseline Business Architecture, if appropriate – this is a description of the existing Business Architecture
- Target Business Architecture, including:
  - Organization structure – identifying business locations and relating them to organizational units
  - Business goals and objectives – for the enterprise and each organizational unit
  - Business functions – a detailed, recursive step involving successive decomposition of major functional areas into sub-functions
  - Business services – the services that the enterprise and each enterprise unit provides to its customers, both internally and externally
  - Business processes, including measures and deliverables
  - Business roles, including development and modification of skills requirements
  - Business data model
  - Correlation of organization and functions – relate business functions to organizational units in the form of a matrix report
- Views corresponding to the selected viewpoints addressing key stakeholder concerns

3.15.2 Information Systems Architectures

The Information Systems Architectures are developed in Phase C. The topics that should be addressed in the Architecture Definition Document related to the Information Systems Architectures are as follows:

- Baseline Data Architecture, if appropriate
- Target Data Architecture, including:
  - Business data model
  - Logical data model
  - Data management process models
  - Data Entity/Business Function matrix
- Data Architecture views corresponding to the selected viewpoints addressing key stakeholder concerns
- Baseline Application Architecture, if appropriate
- Target Application Architecture
- Application Architecture views corresponding to the selected viewpoints addressing key stakeholder concerns

3.15.3 Technology Architecture

The Technology Architecture is developed as part of Phase D. The topics that should be addressed in the Architecture Definition Document related to Technology Architecture are as follows:

- Baseline Technology Architecture, if appropriate
- Target Technology Architecture, including:
  - Technology components and their relationships to information systems
  - Technology platforms and their decomposition, showing the combinations of technology required to realize a particular technology "stack"
  - Environments and locations – a grouping of the required technology into computing environments (e.g., development, production)
  - Expected processing load and distribution of load across technology components
  - Physical (network) communications
  - Hardware and network specifications

- Views corresponding to the selected viewpoints addressing key stakeholder concerns

3.16 Architecture Requirements Specification

The Architecture Requirements Specification provides a set of quantitative statements that outline what an implementation project must do in order to comply with the architecture. An Architecture Requirements Specification will typically form a major component of an implementation contract or contract for more detailed architecture definition.

As mentioned earlier in this chapter, the Architecture Requirements Specification is a companion to the Architecture Definition Document, with a complementary objective to provide the quantitative view.

The following contents are typical within an Architecture Requirements Specification:
- Success measures
- Architecture requirements
- Business service contracts
- Application service contracts
- Implementation guidelines
- Implementation specifications
- Implementation standards
- Interoperability requirements (see Section 3.16.4)
- IT service management requirements
- Constraints
- Assumptions

3.16.1 Business Architecture Requirements

Business Architecture requirements populating the Architecture Requirements Specification in Phase B include:
- Gap analysis results

- Technical requirements
  An initial set of technical requirements should be generated as the
  output of Phase B (Business Architecture). These are the drivers for
  the Technology Architecture work that follows, and should identify,
  categorize, and prioritize the implications for work in the remaining
  architecture domains; for example, by a dependency/priority matrix
  (e.g., guiding trade-off between speed of transaction processing and
  security); list the specific models that are expected to be produced
  (e.g., expressed as primitives of the Zachman Framework).
- Updated business requirements
  The Business Scenarios technique can be used to discover and
  document business requirements.

3.16.2 Information Systems Architectures Requirements
Information Systems Architecture requirements populating the
Architecture Requirements Specification in Phase C include:
- Gap analysis results
- Data interoperability requirements
- Application interoperability requirements
- Areas where the Business Architecture may need to change in order to
  comply with changes in the Data and/or Application Architecture
- Constraints on the Technology Architecture about to be designed
- Updated business requirements, if appropriate
- Updated application requirements, if appropriate
- Updated data requirements, if appropriate

3.16.3 Technology Architecture Requirements
Technology Architecture requirements populating the Architecture
Requirements Specification in Phase D include:
- Gap analysis results
- Updated technology requirements

3.16.4 Interoperability Requirements

The determination of interoperability is present throughout the ADM cycle. A set of guidelines is provided in Part III of the standard, Chapter 25, for defining and establishing interoperability requirements.

3.17 Architecture Roadmap

The Architecture Roadmap lists individual work packages that will realize the Target Architecture and lays them out on a timeline to show progression from the Baseline Architecture to the Target Architecture. The Architecture Roadmap highlights individual work packages' business value at each stage. Transition Architectures necessary to effectively realize the Target Architecture are identified as intermediate steps. The Architecture Roadmap is incrementally developed throughout Phases E and F, and informed by the roadmap components developed in Phases B, C, and D.

The following contents are typically found within an Architecture Roadmap:
- Work package portfolio:
  - Work package description (name, description, objectives, deliverables)
  - Functional requirements
  - Dependencies
  - Relationship to opportunity
  - Relationship to Architecture Definition Document and Architecture Requirements Specification
  - Business Value
- Implementation Factor Assessment and Deduction matrix, including: Risks
  - Issues
  - Assumptions
  - Dependencies
  - Actions
  - Impact

- Consolidated Gaps, Solutions, and Dependencies Matrix, including:
  - Architecture domain
  - Gap
  - Potential solutions
  - Dependencies
- Transition Architectures, if any
- Implementation recommendations:
  - Criteria/measures of effectiveness of projects
  - Risks and issues
  - Solution Building Blocks (SBBs)

3.18 Business Scenarios

The TOGAF standard recommends use of the business scenarios technique[6] for identifying and articulating business requirements. A business scenario is a description of a business problem, which enables requirements to be viewed in relation to one another in the context of the overall problem. Without such a description to serve as context, the business value of solving the problem is unclear, the relevance of potential solutions is unclear, and there is a danger of the solution being based on an inadequate set of requirements.

A key factor in the success of any other major project is the extent to which it is linked to business requirements, and demonstrably supports and enables the enterprise to achieve its business objectives. Business scenarios are an important technique to help identify and understand business needs.

The technique may be used iteratively, at different levels of detail in the hierarchical decomposition of the Business Architecture. The generic business scenario process is as follows:
- Identify, document, and rank the problem that is driving the project

---

6 See TOGAF® Series Guide: Business Scenarios, September 2017 (G176), published by The Open Group; refer to: www.opengroup.org/library/g176.

- Document, as high-level architecture models, the business and technical environments where the problem situation is occurring
- Identify and document desired objectives; the results of handling the problems successfully
- Identify human actors and their place in the business model, the human participants, and their roles
- Identify computer actors and their place in the technology model, the computing elements, and their roles
- Identify and document roles, responsibilities, and measures of success per actor, the required scripts per actor, and the desired results of handling the situation properly
- Check for fitness-for-purpose of inspiring subsequent architecture work, and refine only if necessary

3.19 Gap Analysis

The technique known as gap analysis is widely used in the ADM to validate an architecture that is being developed. It is usually the final step within a phase. The basic premise is to highlight a shortfall between the Baseline Architecture and the Target Architecture; that is, items that have been deliberately omitted, accidentally left out, or not yet defined.

The steps are as follows:
- Draw up a matrix with all the Architecture Building Blocks (ABBs) of the Baseline Architecture on the vertical axis, and all the ABBs of the Target Architecture on the horizontal axis
- Add to the Baseline Architecture axis a final row labeled "New ABBs", and to the Target Architecture axis a final column labeled "Eliminated ABBs"
- Where an ABB is available in both the Baseline and Target Architectures, record this with "Included" at the intersecting cell
- Where an ABB from the Baseline Architecture is missing in the Target Architecture, each must be reviewed
  If it was correctly eliminated, mark it as such in the appropriate "Eliminated" cell. If it was not, you have uncovered an accidental

omission in your Target Architecture that must be addressed by reinstating the ABB in the next iteration of the architecture design – mark it as such in the appropriate "Eliminated" cell.

- Where an ABB from the Target Architecture cannot be found in the Baseline Architecture, mark it at the intersection with the "New" row as a gap that needs to filled, either by developing or procuring the building block

When the exercise is complete, anything under "Eliminated Services" or "New Services" is a gap, which should either be explained as correctly eliminated, or marked as to be addressed by reinstating or developing/procuring the function.

Table 10 shows examples of gaps between the Baseline Architecture and the Target Architecture; in this case the missing elements are "broadcast services" and "shared screen services".

The gap analysis technique should be used in Phases B, C, D, and E of the ADM.

3.20 Architecture Viewpoints

The architect uses architecture views and architecture viewpoints in the ADM cycle during Phases A through D for developing architectures for each domain (Business, Data, Application, and Technology). An architecture view is what you see. An architecture viewpoint is where you are looking from; the vantage point or perspective that determines what you see (an architecture viewpoint can also be thought of as a schema). Architecture viewpoints are generic, and can be stored in libraries for re-use. An architecture view is always specific to the architecture for which it is created. Every architecture view has an associated architecture viewpoint that describes it, at least implicitly.

Table 16: Gap Analysis Example

Target Architecture → Baseline Architecture ↓	Video Conferencing Services	Enhanced Telephony Services	Mailing List Services	Eliminated Services ↓
Broadcast Services				Intentionally Eliminated
Video Conferencing Services	Included			
Enhanced Telephony Services		Potential Match		
Shared Screen Services				Unintentionally excluded – a gap in Target Architecture
New ↓		Gap: Enhanced services to be developed or produced	Gap: Enhanced services to be developed or produced	

ISO/IEC/IEEE 42010:2011 encourages architects to define architecture viewpoints explicitly. Making this distinction between the content and schema of a view may seem at first to be an unnecessary overhead, but it provides a mechanism for re-using architecture viewpoints across different architectures.

To illustrate the concepts of architecture views and architecture viewpoints, consider Example 1. This is a very simple airport system with two different stakeholders: the pilot and the air traffic controller. In this example, the terms view and viewpoint are used as synonyms for architecture view and architecture viewpoint, respectively.

Example 1: Architecture Views and Architecture Viewpoints for a Simple Airport System

Architecture Views and Architecture Viewpoints for a Simple Airport System

The pilot has one view of the system, and the air traffic controller has another. Neither view represents the whole system, because the perspective of each stakeholder constrains (and reduces) how each sees the overall system.

The view of the pilot comprises some elements not viewed by the controller, such as passengers and fuel, while the view of the controller comprises some elements not viewed by the pilot, such as other planes. There are also elements shared between the views, such as the communication model between the pilot and the controller, and the vital information about the plane itself.

A viewpoint is a model (or description) of the information contained in a view. In this example, one viewpoint is the description of how the pilot sees the system, and the other viewpoint is how the controller sees the system. Pilots describe the system from their perspective, using a model of their position and vector toward or away from the runway. All pilots use this model, and the model has a specific language that is used to capture information and populate the model. Controllers describe the system differently, using a model of the airspace and the locations and vectors of aircraft within the airspace. Again, all controllers use a common language derived from the common model in order to capture and communicate information pertinent to their viewpoint.

Fortunately, when controllers talk with pilots, they use a common communication language. (In other words, the models representing their individual viewpoints partially intersect.) Part of this common language is about location and vectors of aircraft, and is essential to safety. So in essence each viewpoint is an abstract model of how all the stakeholders of a particular type – all pilots, or all controllers – view the airport system. The interface to the human user of a tool is typically close to the model and language associated with the viewpoint. The unique tools of the pilot are fuel, altitude, speed, and location indicators. The main tool of the controller is radar. The common tool is a radio.

To summarize from Example 1, we can see that an architecture view can subset the system through the perspective of the stakeholder, such as the pilot *versus* the controller. This subset can be described by an abstract model, called an architecture viewpoint, such as an air flight *versus* an air space model. This description of the architecture view is documented in a partially specialized language, such as "pilot-speak" *versus* "controller-speak". Tools are used to assist the stakeholders, and they interface with each other in terms of the language derived from the architecture viewpoint. When stakeholders use common tools, such as the radio contact between pilot and controller, a common language is essential.

3.21 Architecture Views

Architecture views are representations of the overall architecture that are meaningful to one or more stakeholders in the system. The architect chooses and develops a set of architecture views in the ADM cycle during

Phases A through D that enable the architecture to be communicated to, and understood by, all the stakeholders, and enable them to verify that the system will address their concerns. The concepts in Section 5.3 are central to the use of architecture views within the TOGAF framework.

3.21.1 Developing Views in the ADM

The choice of which particular architecture views to develop is one of the key decisions that the architect has to make.

The architect has a responsibility for ensuring the completeness (fitness-for-purpose) of the architecture, in terms of adequately addressing all the pertinent concerns of its stakeholders; and the integrity of the architecture, in terms of connecting all the various views to each other, satisfactorily reconciling the conflicting concerns of different stakeholders, and showing the trade-offs made in so doing (as between security and performance, for example).

3.22 Architecture Building Blocks

Architecture Building Blocks (ABBs) are architecture documentation and models from the enterprise's Architecture Repository classified according to the Architecture Continuum (see Chapter 6). They are defined or selected during application of the ADM (mainly in Phases A, B, C, and D). The characteristics of ABBs are as follows:

- They capture architecture requirements; e.g., business, data, application, and technology requirements
- They direct and guide the development of Solution Building Blocks (SBBs)

The content of ABB specifications includes the following as a minimum:

- Fundamental functionality and attributes: semantics, unambiguous, including security capability and manageability
- Interfaces: chosen set, supplied (APIs, data formats, protocols, hardware interfaces, standards)

- Interoperability and relationship with other building blocks
- Dependent building blocks with required functionality and named user interfaces
- Map to business/organizational entities and policies

Each ABB should include a statement of any architecture documentation and models from the enterprise's Architecture Repository that can be re-used in the architecture development. The specification of building blocks using the ADM is an evolutionary and iterative process.

See Section 5.5 for further information.

3.23 Solution Building Blocks

Solution Building Blocks (SBBs) relate to the Solutions Continuum. They are implementations of the architectures identified in the enterprise's Architecture Continuum and may be either procured or developed. SBBs appear in Phase E of the ADM where product-specific building blocks are considered for the first time. SBBs define what products and components will implement the functionality, thereby defining the implementation. They fulfill business requirements and are product or vendor-aware. The content of an SBB specification includes the following as a minimum:

- Specific functionality and attributes
- Interfaces; the implemented set
- Required SBBs used with required functionality and names of the interfaces used
- Mapping from the SBBs to the IT topology and operational policies
- Specifications of attributes shared such as security, manageability, localizability, scalability
- Performance, configurability
- Design drivers and constraints, including the physical architecture
- Relationships between the SBBs and ABBs

3.24 Capability-Based Planning

Phases E and F feature a detailed method for defining and planning enterprise transformation based on the principles of capability-based planning, a business planning technique that focuses on business outcomes. It is business-driven and business-led and combines the requisite efforts of all lines of business to achieve the desired capability. It accommodates most, if not all, of the corporate business models and is especially useful in organizations where a latent capability to respond (e.g., an emergency preparedness unit) is required and the same resources are involved in multiple capabilities. Often the need for these capabilities is discovered and refined using business scenarios.

Figure 5 illustrates the relationship between capability-based planning, Enterprise Architecture, and portfolio/project management.

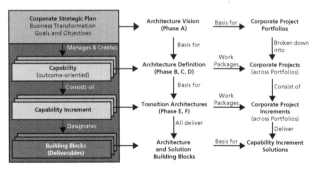

Figure 5: Relationship between Capabilities, Enterprise Architecture, and Projects

3.25 Migration Planning Techniques

A number of techniques are provided to support migration planning in Phases E and F. These are described in the following sections.

3.25.1 Implementation Factor Assessment and Deduction Matrix

The technique of creating an Implementation Factor Assessment and Deduction Matrix is used in Phase E to document factors having an impact on the architecture Implementation and Migration Plan. The matrix should include a list of the factors, their descriptions, and the deductions (conclusions) that indicate the actions or constraints that have to be taken into consideration when formulating the plans.

Typical factors include risks, issues, assumptions, dependencies, actions, and impacts.

An example matrix is shown in Table 11.

Table 11: Implementation Factor Assessment and Deduction Matrix

Implementation Factor Assessment and Deduction Matrix		
Factor	Description	Deduction
<Name of the Factor>	<Description of the Factor>	<Impact on the Migration Plan>
Change in Technology	Shut down the message centers, saving 700 personnel, and have them replaced by email	Need for personnel training, re-assignment Email has major personnel savings and should be given priority.
Consolidation of Services	...	...
Introduction of New Customer Service	...	...

3.25.2 Consolidated Gaps, Solutions, and Dependencies Matrix

The technique of creating a Consolidated Gaps, Solutions, and Dependencies Matrix allows the architect to group the gaps identified in the domain architecture gap analysis results and assess potential solutions and dependencies to one or more gaps. An example is shown in Table 12. This matrix can be used as a planning tool when creating work packages. The identified dependencies drive the creation of projects and migration planning in Phases E and F.

Table 12: Consolidated Gaps, Solutions, and Dependencies Matrix

Consolidated Gaps, Solutions, and Dependencies Matrix				
#	Architecture	Gap	Potential Solutions	Dependencies
1	Business	New Order Processing Process	Use COTS software tool process Implement custom solution	Drives Application #2
2	Application	New Order Processing Application	COTS software tool X Develop in-house	
3	Information	Consolidated Customer Information Base	Use COTS customer base Develop customer data mart	

3.25.3 Architecture Definition Increments Table

The technique of creating an Architecture Definition Increments Table allows the architect to plan a series of Transition Architectures outlining the status of the Enterprise Architecture at specified times. A table should be drawn up, as shown in Table 13, listing the projects and then assigning their incremental deliverables across the Transition Architectures.

Table 13: Example Architecture Definition Increments Table

Architecture Definition: Project Objectives by Increment				
Project	April 2017/2018 Transitional Architecture 1: Preparation	April 2018/2020 Transitional Architecture 2: Initial Operational Capability	April 2020/2021 Transitional Architecture 3: Benefits	Comments
Enterprise e-Services Capability	Training and Business Process	e-licensing Capability	e-employment Benefits	
IT e-Forms	Design and Build			
IT e-Information Environment	Design and Build Information Environment	Client Common Data Web Content Design and Build	Enterprise Common Data Document Management Design and Build	
...	...	...	...	...

3.25.4 Transition Architecture State Evolution Table

The technique of creating the Transition Architecture State Evolution Table allows the architect to show the proposed state of the architectures at various levels using the defined taxonomy (e.g., the TOGAF TRM).

A table should be drawn, listing the services from the taxonomy used in the enterprise, the Transition Architectures, and proposed transformations, as shown in Table 14.

All Solution Building Blocks (SBBs) should be described with respect to their delivery and impact on these services. They should also be marked to show the progression of the Enterprise Architecture. In the example, where target capability has been reached, this is shown as "new" or "retain"; where capability is transitioned to a new solution, this is marked as "transition"; and where a capability is to be replaced, this is marked as "replace".

Table 14: Example Transition Architecture State Evolution Table

Architectural State Using the Technical Reference Model				
Sub-Domain	Service	Transition Architecture 1	Transition Architecture 2	Transition Architecture 3
Infrastructure Applications	Information Exchange Services	Solution System A (replace)	Solution System B-1 (transition)	Solution System B-2 (new)
	Data Management Services	Solution System D (retain)	Solution System D (retain)	Solution System D (retain)
…	…			

3.25.5 Business Value Assessment Technique

A technique to assess business value is to draw up a matrix based on a value index dimension and a risk index dimension. An example is shown in Figure 6. The value index should include criteria such as compliance

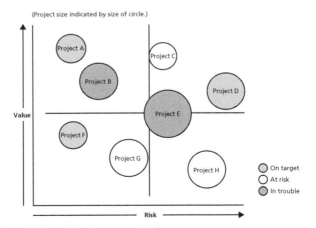

Figure 6: Business Value Assessment Matrix

to principles, financial contribution, strategic alignment, and competitive position. The risk index should include criteria such as size and complexity, technology, organizational capacity, and impact of a failure. Each criterion should be assigned an individual weight.

The index and its criteria and weighting should be developed and approved by senior management. It is important to establish the decision-making criteria before the options are known.

3.26 Implementation and Migration Plan

The Implementation and Migration Plan is developed in Phases E and F, and provides a schedule of the projects for implementation of the Target Architecture. The Implementation and Migration Plan includes executable projects grouped into managed portfolios and programs. The Implementation and Migration Strategy identifying the approach to change is a key element of the Implementation and Migration Plan.

Typical contents are as follows:
- Implementation and Migration Strategy:
  - Strategic Implementation Direction
  - Implementation Sequencing Approach
- Project and portfolio breakdown of implementation:
  - Allocation of work packages to project and portfolio
  - Capabilities delivered by projects
  - Milestones and timing
  - Work breakdown structure
  - May include impact on existing portfolio, program, and projects

It may contain:
- Project charters:
  - Included work packages
  - Business value
  - Risk, issues, assumptions, dependencies
  - Resource requirements and costs

- Benefits of migration, determined (including mapping to business requirements)
- Estimated costs of migration options

3.27 Transition Architecture

Where the scope of change to implement the Target Architecture requires an incremental approach, one or more Transition Architectures are defined within the Architecture Definition Document output from Phase E. A Transition Architecture shows the enterprise at an architecturally significant state between the Baseline and Target Architectures. Transition Architectures are used to describe transitional Target Architectures necessary for effective realization of the Target Architecture. These provide an ability to identify clear targets along the roadmap to realizing the Target Architecture.

The following contents are typical within a Transition Architecture:
- Transition Architecture:
  - Definition of transition states
  - Business Architecture for each transition state
  - Data Architecture for each transition state
  - Application Architecture for each transition state
  - Technology Architecture for each transition state

3.28 Implementation Governance Model

Once an architecture has been defined, it is necessary to plan how the Transition Architecture that implements the architecture will be governed through implementation. Within organizations that have established architecture functions, there is likely to be a governance framework already in place, but specific processes, organizations, roles, responsibilities, and measures may need to be defined on a project-by-project basis.

The Implementation Governance Model produced as an output of Phase F ensures that a project transitioning into implementation also smoothly transitions into appropriate Architecture Governance (for Phase G).

Typical contents of an Implementation Governance Model are:
- Governance processes
- Governance organization structure
- Governance roles and responsibilities
- Governance checkpoints and success/failure criteria

3.29 Architecture Contracts

Architecture Contracts are produced in Phase G: Implementation Governance. Architecture Contracts are the joint agreements between development partners and sponsors on the deliverables, quality, and fitness-for-purpose of an architecture. Successful implementation of these agreements will be delivered through effective architecture. By implementing a governed approach to the management of contracts, the following will be ensured:
- A system of continuous monitoring to check integrity, changes, decision-making, and audit of all architecture-related activities within the organization
- Adherence to the principles, standards, and requirements of the existing or developing architectures
- Identification of risks in all aspects of the development and implementation of the architecture(s) covering the internal development against accepted standards, policies, technologies, and products as well as the operational aspects of the architectures such that the organization can continue its business within a resilient environment
- A set of processes and practices that ensure accountability, responsibility, and discipline with regard to the development and usage of all architectural artifacts

- A formal understanding of the governance organization responsible for the contract, their level of authority, and scope of the architecture under the governance of this body

The TOGAF standard identifies two example contracts as follows:
- Architecture Design and Development Contract
- Business Users' Architecture Contract

Typical contents of an Architecture Design and Development Contract are:
- Introduction and background
- The nature of the agreement
- Scope of the architecture
- Architecture and strategic principles and requirements
- Conformance requirements
- Architecture development and management process and roles
- Target Architecture measures
- Defined phases of deliverables
- Prioritized joint work plan
- Time window(s)
- Architecture delivery and business metrics

Typical contents of a Business Users' Architecture Contract produced in Phase G are:
- Introduction and background
- The nature of the agreement
- Scope
- Strategic requirements
- Conformance requirements
- Architecture adopters
- Time window
- Architecture business metrics
- Service architecture (includes Service Level Agreement (SLA))

This contract is also used to manage changes to the Enterprise Architecture in Phase H.

3.30 Change Request

Requests for Architecture Change are considered in Phase H: Architecture Change Management.

During implementation of an architecture, as more facts become known, it is possible that the original architecture definition and requirements are not suitable or are not sufficient to complete the implementation of a solution. In these circumstances, it is necessary for implementation projects to either deviate from the suggested architectural approach or to request scope extensions. Additionally, external factors – such as market factors, changes in business strategy, and new technology opportunities – may open up opportunities to extend and refine the architecture.

In these circumstances, a Change Request may be submitted in order to kick-start a further cycle of architecture work.

Typical contents of a Change Request are:
- Description of the proposed change
- Rationale for the proposed change
- Impact assessment of the proposed change, including:
  - Reference to specific requirements
  - Stakeholder priority of the requirements to date
  - Phases to be revisited
  - Phase to lead on requirements prioritization
  - Results of phase investigations and revised priorities
  - Recommendations on management of requirements
- Repository reference number

3.31 Compliance Assessment

Once an architecture has been defined, it is necessary to govern that architecture through implementation to ensure that the original Architecture Vision is appropriately realized and that any implementation lessons are fed back into the architecture process. Periodic compliance reviews of implementation projects in Phase G provide a mechanism to review project progress and ensure that the design and implementation is proceeding in-line with the strategic and architectural objectives.

Typical contents of a Compliance Assessment are:
- Overview of project progress and status
- Overview of project architecture/design
- Completed architecture checklists:
  - Hardware and operating system checklist
  - Software services and middleware checklist
  - Applications checklists
  - Information management checklists
  - Security checklists
  - System management checklists
  - System engineering checklists
  - Methods and tools checklists

3.32 Requirements Impact Assessment

Throughout the ADM, new information is collected relating to an architecture. As this information is gathered, new facts may come to light that invalidate existing aspects of the architecture. A Requirements Impact Assessment assesses the current architecture requirements and specification to identify changes that should be made and the implications of those changes.

It documents an assessment of the changes and the recommendations for change to the architecture. The recommended contents are as follows:
- Reference to specific requirements
- Stakeholder priority of the requirements to date
- Phases to be revisited
- Phase to lead on requirements prioritization

- Results of phase investigations and revised priorities
- Recommendations on management of requirements
- Repository reference number

These are often produced as a response to a Change Request.

Chapter 4
Guidelines for Adapting the ADM

This chapter provides guidelines for adapting the ADM.

4.1 Introduction

The ADM is a generic method for architecture development, which is designed to deal with most system and organizational requirements. However, it will often be necessary to modify or extend the ADM to suit specific needs. One of the tasks before applying the ADM is to review the process and its outputs for applicability, and then tailor them as appropriate to the circumstances of the individual enterprise. This activity may well produce an "enterprise-specific" ADM.

There are a number of reasons for wanting to tailor the ADM to the circumstances of an individual enterprise. Some of the reasons are outlined as follows:

1. An important consideration is that the order of the phases in the ADM is to some extent dependent on the maturity of the architecture discipline within the enterprise concerned. For example, if the business case for doing architecture is not well recognized, then creating an Architecture Vision is essential; and a detailed Business Architecture needs to come next to define the business case for the remaining architecture work, and secure the active participation of key stakeholders in that work.

2. The order of phases may also be defined by the Business and Architecture Principles of an enterprise. For example, the business principles may dictate that the enterprise be prepared to adjust its business processes to meet the needs of a packaged solution, so that it can be implemented quickly to enable fast response to market changes. In such a case, the Business Architecture (or at least the completion

of it) may well follow completion of the Information Systems Architecture.

3. An enterprise may wish to use or tailor the ADM in conjunction with another Enterprise Architecture framework that has a defined set of deliverables specific to a particular vertical sector: Government, Defense, e-Business, Telecommunications, etc.

4. The ADM is one of many corporate processes that make up the corporate governance model for an enterprise. The ADM is complementary to, and supportive of, other standard program management processes. The enterprise will tailor the ADM to reflect the relationships with, and dependencies on, the other management processes.

5. The ADM is being mandated for use by a prime or lead contractor in an outsourcing situation, and needs to be tailored to achieve a suitable compromise between the contractor's existing practices and the contracting enterprise's requirements.

6. The enterprise is a small-to-medium enterprise, and wishes to use a "cut-down" version of the ADM that is more attuned to the reduced level of resources and system complexity typical of such an environment.

7. The enterprise is very large and complex, comprising many separate but interlinked "enterprises" within an overall collaborative business framework, and the architecture method needs to be adapted to recognize this situation. Such enterprises usually cannot be treated successfully as a single entity and a more federated approach is required.

The ADM process can also be adapted to deal with a number of different use scenarios, including different process styles (e.g., the use of iteration) and also specific specialist architectures (such as security). These are discussed in the following sections.

4.2 Applying Iteration to the ADM

The ADM supports a number of concepts that could be characterized as iteration.

Iteration to develop a comprehensive Architecture Landscape:

- Projects will iterate through the entire ADM cycle, commencing with Phase A
  Each cycle of the ADM will be bound by a Request for Architecture Work. The architecture output will populate the Architecture Landscape, either extending the landscape described, or changing the landscape where required.
- Separate projects may operate their own ADM cycles concurrently, with relationships between the different projects
- One project may trigger the initiation of another project
  Typically, this is used when higher-level architecture initiatives identify opportunities or solutions that require more detailed architecture, or when a project identifies landscape impacts outside the scope of its Request for Architecture Work.

Iteration within an ADM cycle:

- Projects may operate multiple ADM phases concurrently
  Typically, this is used to manage the inter-relationship between Business Architecture, Information Systems Architecture, and Technology Architecture.
- Projects may cycle between ADM phases, in planned cycles covering multiple phases
  Typically, this is used to converge on a detailed Target Architecture when higher-level architecture does not exist to provide context and constraint.
- Projects may return to previous phases in order to circle back and update work products with new information
  Typically, this is used to converge on an executable Architecture Roadmap or Implementation and Migration Plan, when the

implementation details and scope of change trigger a change or re-prioritization of stakeholder requirements.

Iteration to manage the Architecture Capability:
- The result of addressing a Request for Architecture Work in Phase A may require a new iteration of the Preliminary Phase to adjust the Architecture Capability for the organization
- Changes identified in Phase H may require a new iteration of the Preliminary Phase to adjust the Architecture Capability for the organization

All of these techniques are valid applications of the ADM and can be used to ensure that the approach to architecture development is sufficiently flexible to accommodate other methods and frameworks.

The TOGAF standard includes consideration of the organizational factors that influence the extent to which the ADM should be used in an iterative fashion, different styles of iteration, and a mapping of ADM phases to iteration cycles for architecture definition.

A suggested iteration cycle for iterations that span multiple ADM phases is shown in Figure 7.

- **Architecture Capability** iterations support the creation and evolution of the required Architecture Capability
  This cycle includes the initial mobilization of the architecture activity for a given purpose or architecture engagement type by establishing or adjusting the architecture approach, principles, scope, vision, and governance.
- **Architecture Development** iterations allow creation of content by cycling through, or integrating, Business, Information Systems, and Technology Architecture phases
  These iterations ensure that the architecture is considered as a whole. In this type of iteration stakeholder reviews are typically broader. As

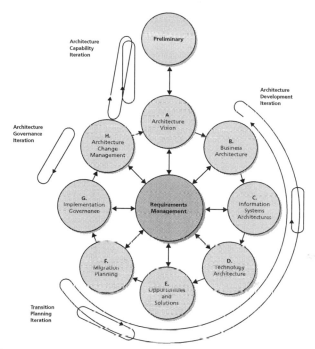

Figure 7: Iteration Cycles

the iterations converge on a target, extensions into the Opportunities and Solutions and Migration Planning phases ensure that the architecture's implementability is considered as the architecture is finalized.

- **Transition Planning** iterations support the creation of formal change roadmaps for a defined architecture
- **Architecture Governance** iterations support governance of change activity progressing towards a defined Target Architecture

The TOGAF standard defines two styles of architecture definition:

- **Baseline First** – in this style, the Baseline Architecture is assessed first
  This process is suitable when a target solution is not clearly
  understood.

TOGAF Phase		Architecture Development			Transition Planning		Architecture Governance	
		Iteration 1	Iteration 2	Iteration n	Iteration 1	Iteration n	Iteration 1	Iteration n
Preliminary		Informal	Informal	Informal	Informal	Informal		Light
Architecture Vision		Informal	Informal	Informal	Informal	Informal		Light
Business Architecture	Baseline	Core	Light	Core	Informal	Informal		Light
	Target	Informal	Core	Core	Informal	Informal		Light
Application Architecture	Baseline	Core	Light	Core	Informal	Informal		Light
	Target	Informal	Core	Core	Informal	Informal		Light
Data Architecture	Baseline	Core	Light	Core	Informal	Informal		Light
	Target	Informal	Core	Core	Informal	Informal		Light
Technology Architecture	Baseline	Core	Light	Core	Informal	Informal		Light
	Target	Informal	Core	Core	Informal	Informal		Light
Opportunities and Solutions		Light	Light	Light	Core	Core	Informal	Informal
Migration Planning		Light	Light		Core	Core	Informal	Informal
Implementation Governance					Informal	Informal	Core	Core
Change Management		Informal	Informal	Informal	Informal	Informal	Core	Core

Core: primary focus activity for the iteration

Light: secondary focus activity for the iteration

Informal: potential activity for the iteration, not formally mentioned in the method

Figure 8: Activity by Iteration for Baseline First Architecture Definition

- **Target First**: In this style, the Target Architecture is elaborated in detail and then mapped back to the baseline, in order to define change activity

TOGAF Phase		Architecture Development			Transition Planning		Architecture Governance	
		Iteration 1	Iteration 2	Iteration n	Iteration 1	Iteration n	Iteration 1	Iteration n
Preliminary		Informal	Informal	Informal	Informal	Informal		Light
Architecture Vision		Informal	Informal	Informal	Informal	Informal		Light
Business Architecture	Baseline	Informal	Core	Core	Informal	Informal		Light
	Target	Core	Light	Core	Informal	Informal		Light
Application Architecture	Baseline	Informal	Core	Core	Informal	Informal		Light
	Target	Core	Light	Core	Informal	Informal		Light
Data Architecture	Baseline	Informal	Core	Core	Informal	Informal		Light
	Target	Core	Light	Core	Informal	Informal		Light
Technology Architecture	Baseline	Informal	Core	Core	Informal	Informal		Light
	Target	Core	Light	Core	Informal	Informal		Light
Opportunities and Solutions		Light	Light	Light	Core	Core	Informal	Informal
Migration Planning		Light	Light	Light	Core	Core	Informal	Informal
Implementation Governance					Informal	Informal	Core	Core
Change Management		Informal	Informal	Informal	Informal	Informal	Core	Core

Core: primary focus activity for the iteration

Light: secondary focus activity for the iteration

Informal: potential activity for the iteration, not formally mentioned in the method

Figure 9: Activity by Iteration for Target First Architecture Definition

This process is suitable when a target state is agreed at a high level and the enterprise wishes to avoid proliferating current business practice into the target.

The TOGAF standard maps both styles to iteration cycles, as illustrated in Figure 8 and Figure 9.

The TOGAF standard also describes a hierarchical application of iteration where each ADM cycle occurs at a single level of architecture description. This approach to the ADM uses the Migration Planning phase of one ADM cycle to initiate new, more detailed architecture projects, which will also develop architectures. This type of iteration highlights the need for higher-level architecture to guide and constrain more detailed architecture. It also highlights that the complete Architecture Landscape is developed by multiple ADM iterations. This approach is shown in Figure 10.

4.3 Applying the ADM across the Architecture Landscape

In a typical enterprise, many architectures will be described in the Architecture Landscape at any point in time. Some architectures will address very specific needs; others will be more general. Some will address detail; some will provide a big picture. To address this complexity the TOGAF standard uses the concepts of levels and the Enterprise Continuum to provide a conceptual framework for organizing the Architecture Landscape.

Levels provide a framework for dividing the Architecture Landscape into three levels of granularity:

1. **Strategic Architecture** provides an organizing framework for operational and change activity and allows for direction setting at an executive level.

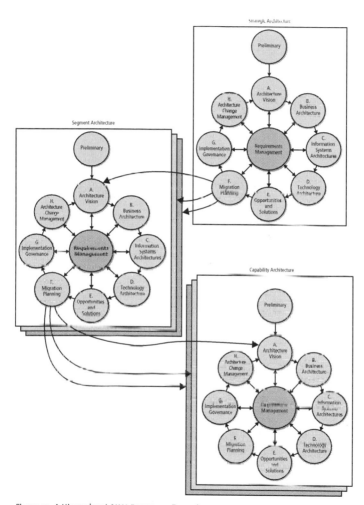

Figure 10: A Hierarchy of ADM Processes Example

2. **Segment Architecture** provides an organizing framework for operational and change activity and allows for direction setting and the development of effective architecture roadmaps at a program or portfolio level.
3. **Capability Architecture** provides an organizing framework for change activity and the development of effective architecture roadmaps realizing capability increments.

Figure 11 shows a summary of the classification model for Architecture Landscapes.

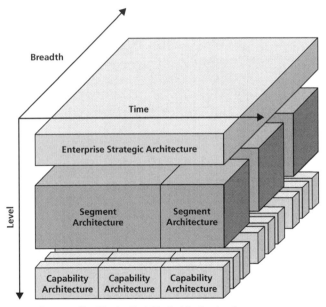

Figure 11: Summary Classification Model for Architecture Landscape

The TOGAF standard describes the types of engagement that architects may be required to perform and how the ADM can be used to coordinate activities of various teams of architects working at different levels. It also provides two strategies for using the ADM as a process to support hierarchies of architectures:

- Architectures at different levels can be developed through iterations within a single ADM process
- Architectures at different levels can be developed through a hierarchy of ADM processes executed concurrently

At the extreme ends of the scale, either of these two options can be fully adopted. In practice, an architect is likely to need to blend elements of each to fit the exact requirements of their Request for Architecture Work.

4.4 Using the ADM with Different Architectural Styles

Architectural styles differ in terms of focus, form, techniques, materials, subject, and time period. Some styles can be considered as fashionable, others focused on particular aspects of Enterprise Architecture. The TOGAF standard, and its ADM, are designed to be generic and intended for use in a wide variety of environments. They can be readily adapted to a number of architectural styles.

Many architectural styles have been developed to address key problems facing practitioners and to demonstrate how the TOGAF framework can be made more relevant within defined contexts. These are included in the TOGAF Library. Some of these have been developed by The Open Group Forums and Work Groups working in specific areas and have been published in Guides, White Papers, and Standards. Examples include:

- TOGAF® Series Guide: Using the TOGAF® Framework to Define and Govern Service- Oriented Architectures
- Integrating Risk and Security within a TOGAF® Enterprise Architecture

Some of these have been developed collaboratively between The Open Group and other bodies. Examples include:

- TOGAF® and SABSA® Integration
- Integrating the TOGAF® Standard with the BIAN Service Landscape
- Exploring Synergies between TOGAF® and Frameworx
- TOGAF® 9 and DoDAF 2.0

Chapter 5
Architecture Content Framework

This chapter provides an introduction to the Architecture Content Framework, a structured metamodel for architectural artifacts.

5.1 Architecture Content Framework Overview

During the execution of the ADM a number of outputs will be produced as a result, such as process flows, architectural requirements, project plans, project compliance assessments, etc. In order to be able to collate and present these major work products in a consistent and structured manner, it is necessary to have an Architecture Content Framework within which to place them. This allows for easier reference and standard classification, and also to help facilitate the structuring of relationships between the various constituent work products that make up what is often referred to as the "Enterprise Architecture".

The Architecture Content Framework provided is intended to allow the TOGAF framework to be used as a stand-alone framework for architecture within an enterprise. However, other content frameworks exist (such as those provided by the ArchiMate Specification and the Zachman Framework) and it is expected that some enterprises may opt to use an external framework in conjunction with the ADM instead. In these cases, the TOGAF Architecture Content Framework provides a useful reference and starting point for TOGAF content to be mapped to the metamodels of other frameworks.

In order to assist with the classification of new work products and the potential need to correlate with other content frameworks (including any existing classified architecture work products), the Architecture Content

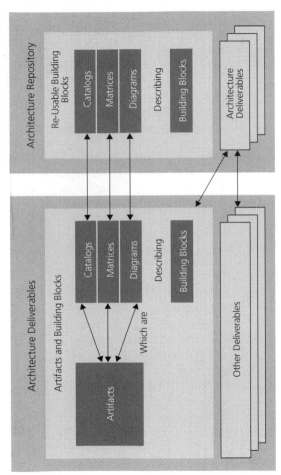

Figure 12: Relationships between Deliverables, Artifacts, and Building Blocks

Framework uses the following three categories to describe the type of architectural work product within its context of use:

- A **deliverable** is a work product that is contractually specified, and would normally be reviewed, agreed, and signed off by its stakeholders – deliverables often represent the output of projects
- An **artifact** is an architectural work product that describes an aspect of the architecture

  Artifacts are generally classified as catalogs (lists of things), matrices (showing relationships between things), and diagrams (pictures of things). Examples include a requirements catalog, business interaction matrix, and a use-case diagram. An architectural deliverable may contain many artifacts and artifacts will form the content of the Architecture Repository.
- A **building block** represents a (potentially re-usable) component of business, IT, or architectural capability that can be combined with other building blocks to deliver architectures and solutions

Building blocks can be defined at various levels of detail and can relate to both "architectures" and "solutions", with Architecture Building Blocks (ABBs) typically describing the required capability in order to shape the Solution Building Blocks (SBBs) which would represent the components to be used to implement the required capability. These are discussed further in Section 5.5.

The relationships between deliverables, artifacts, and building blocks are shown in Figure 12.

5.2 Content Metamodel

The Architecture Content Framework is based upon a standard content metamodel which provides a definition for all the types of building blocks that exist within an architecture. A high-level overview of the content metamodel is shown in Figure 13. The metamodel illustrates how these building blocks can be described and how they relate to one another.

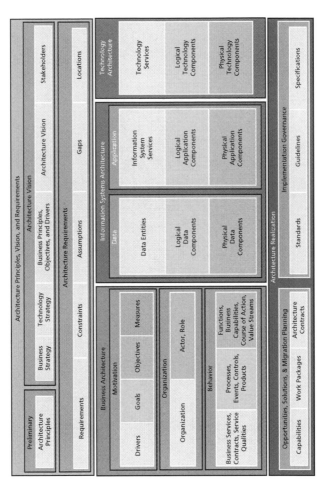

Figure 13: Content Metamodel Overview

When creating and managing architectures, it is necessary to consider various concerns such as business services, actors, applications, data entities, and technology. The content metamodel highlights these concerns, shows their relationships, and identifies artifacts that can be used to represent them in a consistent, structured manner.

Additionally, the content metamodel can be used to provide guidance to any organizations that wish to implement their architecture using an architecture tool.

5.2.1 Core and Extensions

The model has been structured to consider core and extension content, where the core metamodel provides a minimum set of architectural content that supports traceability across artifacts, and extensions are plugged in to support any more specific or in-depth modeling that may be required.

Extensions allow focus in areas of specific interest. All extension modules are optional and should be selected during the Preliminary Phase of the ADM iteration to meet the needs of the organization. The extensions described in the TOGAF standard are for guidance and can be added to or tailored accordingly.

5.3 Architectural Artifacts

The TOGAF standard describes the terminology surrounding the architecture artifacts and then describes the artifacts recommended to be created for each phase within the ADM.

5.3.1 Basic Concepts

The basic concepts and terminology used in this section have been adapted from ISO/IEC/IEEE 42010:2011 and ISO/IEC/IEEE 15288:2015,[7] described in Table 15 and illustrated in Figure 14.[8]

Table 15: Concepts Related to Architecture Views

Concept	Definition
System	A combination of interacting elements organized to achieve one or more stated purposes.
Architecture	The fundamental concepts or properties of a system in its environment embodied in its elements, relationships, and in the principles of its design and evolution.
Architecture Description	A work product used to express an architecture; a collection of architecture views and models that together document the architecture.
Stakeholder	An individual, team, organization, or class thereof, having an interest in a system.
Concern	An interest in a system relevant to one or more of its stakeholders. Concerns may pertain to any aspect of the system's functioning, development, or operation, including considerations such as performance, reliability, security, distribution, and evolvability.
Architecture View	A representation of a system from the perspective of a related set of concerns.
Architecture Viewpoint	A specification of the conventions for a particular kind of architecture view.

7 ISO/IEC/IEEE 15288:2015: Systems and Software Engineering – System Life Cycle Processes.
8 Reprinted with permission from Figure 2 of ISO/IEC/IEEE 42010: 2011, Systems and Software Engineering — Architecture Description, with permission from IEEE. Copyright © 2011, by IEEE. The IEEE disclaims any responsibility or liability resulting from the placement and use in the described manner.

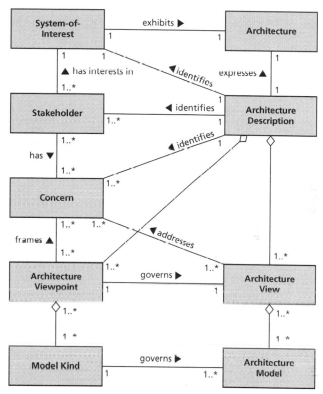

Figure 14: Basic Concepts for Architectural Description

5.3.2 Catalogs, Matrices, and Diagrams

While the content metamodel is used to support the structuring of architectural information, most stakeholders do not need or wish to know the detail contained within the Architecture Content Framework in this manner. Therefore, the use of catalogs, matrices, and diagrams is introduced to facilitate the presentation of architectural information so that it may be used for reference and governance purposes more readily.

Catalogs are lists of building blocks of a specific type or related types, matrices are grids that show relationships between two or more entities, and diagrams are graphical renderings of architectural content.

In summary, the result of an ADM developed architecture consists of a number of defined ABBs populated into architecture catalogs, with relationships specified between those building blocks in architecture matrices, and/or also presented as diagrams, as appropriate to satisfy the stakeholder concerns.

The TOGAF standard provides a set of recommended artifacts, summarized in Table 16.

Table 16: Recommended Artifacts by ADM Phase

ADM Phase	Artifact
Preliminary Phase	Principles catalog
Phase A	Stakeholder Map matrix Value Chain diagram Solution Concept diagram Business Model diagram Business Capability map Value Stream map
Phase B	Organization/Actor catalog Driver/Goal/Objective catalog Role catalog Business Service/Function catalog Location catalog Process/Event/Control/Product catalog Contract/Measure catalog Business Capabilities catalog Value Stream catalog Value Stream Stages catalog Business Interaction matrix

ADM Phase	Artifact
	Actor/Role matrix
	Value Stream/Capability matrix
	Strategy/Capability matrix
	Capability/Organization matrix
	Business Footprint diagram
	Business Service/Information diagram
	Functional Decomposition diagram
	Product Lifecycle diagram
	Goal/Objective/Service diagram
	Business Use-Case diagram
	Organization Decomposition diagram
	Process Flow diagram
	Event diagram
	Business Capability map (updated)
	Value Stream map (updated)
	Organization map
Phase C: Data Architecture	Data Entity/Data Component catalog
	Data Entity/Business Function matrix
	Application/Data matrix
	Conceptual Data Diagram
	Logical Data Diagram
	Data Dissemination diagram
	Data Security diagram
	Data Migration diagram
	Data Lifecycle diagram
Phase C: Application Architecture	Application Portfolio catalog
	Interface catalog
	Application/Organization matrix
	Role/Application matrix
	Application/Function matrix
	Application Interaction matrix
	Application Communication diagram
	Application and User Location diagram
	Application Use-Case diagram
	Enterprise Manageability diagram
	Process/Application Realization diagram
	Software Engineering diagram
	Application Migration diagram
	Software Distribution diagram

ADM Phase	Artifact
Phase D	Technology Standards catalog Technology Portfolio catalog Application/Technology matrix Environments and Locations diagram Platform Decomposition diagram Processing diagram Networked Computing/Hardware diagram Network and Communications diagram
Phase E	Project Context diagram Benefits diagram
Requirements Management	Requirements catalog

5.4 Architecture Deliverables

Part IV of the standard, Chapter 32 provides a typical baseline of
architecture deliverables in order to better define the activities required in
the ADM and act as a starting point for tailoring within an organization.
For details, see Chapter 3.

5.5 Building Blocks

The TOGAF standard includes Architecture Building Blocks (ABBs) and
Solution Building Blocks (SBBs).

A building block is simply a package of functionality defined to meet
business needs. The way in which functionality, products, and custom
developments are assembled into building blocks will vary widely
between individual architectures. Every organization must decide for
itself what arrangement of building blocks works best. A good choice of
building blocks can lead to improvements in legacy system integration,
interoperability, and flexibility in the creation of new systems and
applications.

Systems are built up from collections of building blocks, so most
building blocks have to interoperate with other building blocks.

Wherever that is true, it is important that the interfaces to a building block are published and reasonably stable.

Building blocks can be defined at various levels of detail, depending on what stage of architecture development has been reached.

For instance, at an early stage, a building block can simply consist of a grouping of functionality, such as a customer database and some retrieval tools. Building blocks at this functional level of definition are described as Architecture Building Blocks (ABBs); see Section 3.22. Later on, real products or custom developments replace these simple definitions of functionality, and the building blocks are then described as Solution Building Blocks (SBBs); see Section 3.23.

The key phases and steps of the ADM at which building blocks are evolved and specified are summarized as follows, and illustrated in Figure 15.

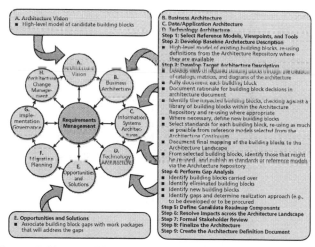

Figure 15: Architecture Building Blocks and their Use in the ADM Cycle

In Phase A, the earliest building block definitions start as relatively abstract entities within the Architecture Vision.

In Phases B, C, and D building blocks within the Business, Data, Application, and Technology Architectures are evolved to a common pattern of steps.

Finally, in Phase E the building blocks become more implementation-specific as SBBs are identified to address gaps.

Chapter 6
The Enterprise Continuum

This chapter provides an introduction to the Enterprise Continuum. Topics addressed in this chapter include:

- An explanation of the Enterprise Continuum and its purpose
- Using the Enterprise Continuum in developing an Enterprise Architecture
- An overview of characteristics to classify and partition architectures
- An overview of a structural framework for an Architecture Repository

6.1 Overview of the Enterprise Continuum

The Enterprise Continuum, shown in Figure 16, provides a model for structuring a "virtual" repository and provides methods for classifying architecture and solution artifacts, showing how different artifacts evolve and how they can be re-used. It is populated with architecture assets and their possible solutions (models, patterns, architecture descriptions, etc.). These assets and solutions can be drawn from within the enterprise or from the industry at large and used in constructing architectures.

A distinction is made between architectures and their possible solutions, thus creating an Architecture Continuum and a Solutions Continuum. As shown in Figure 16, the relationship between them is one of guidance and support.

The Enterprise Continuum supports two general ideas: re-use where possible, especially the avoidance of re-invention, and an aid to communication. The assets in both the Architecture and Solutions Continuums are structured from generic to specific in order to provide a consistent language to effectively communicate the differences between architectures. Understanding where you are in the continuum helps everyone to communicate effectively. Use of the Enterprise Continuum can eliminate ambiguity when discussing concepts and items amongst

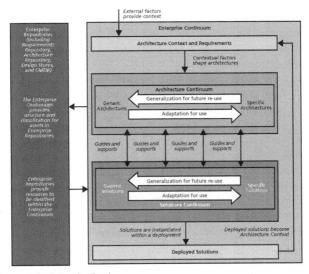

Figure 16: The Enterprise Continuum

different departments within the same organization or even different organizations building Enterprise Architectures. Understanding the architecture helps to better understand the solution. Being able to explain the general concept behind a solution makes it easier to understand possible conflicts.

Since the use of the Enterprise Continuum is usually accompanied by an increase of associated architecture and solution assets, organizations can directly benefit from re-use.

6.1.1 The Enterprise Continuum and Architecture Re-Use

Examples of assets "within the enterprise" are the deliverables of previous architecture work, which are available for re-use. Examples of assets "in the IT industry at large" are the wide variety of industry reference models and architecture patterns that exist, and are continually emerging, including those that are highly generic (such as the TOGAF Technical Reference Model (TRM) from the TOGAF Library); those specific to certain aspects of IT (such as a web services architecture); those specific to certain types of information processing (such as e-Commerce); and those specific to certain vertical industries (such as the ARTS data model from the retail industry). The decision as to which architecture assets a specific enterprise considers part of its own Enterprise Continuum will normally form part of the overall Architecture Governance function within the enterprise concerned.

6.1.2 Using the Enterprise Continuum within the ADM

The TOGAF ADM describes the process of developing an enterprise-specific architecture and an enterprise-specific solution which conform to that architecture by adopting and adapting (where appropriate) generic architectures and solutions. In a similar fashion, specific architectures and solutions that prove to be credible and effective will be generalized for re-use. At relevant places throughout the ADM, there are reminders to consider which architecture assets the architect should use. The TOGAF Library provides reference models for consideration for use in developing an organization's architecture.

6.2 Architecture Partitioning

Partitions are used to simplify the development and management of the Enterprise Architecture. Partitions lie at the foundation of Architecture Governance and are distinct from levels and the organizing concepts of the Architecture Continuum.

Architectures are partitioned because:
- Organizational unit architectures conflict with one another
- Different teams need to work on different elements of architecture at the same time and partitions allow for specific groups of architects to own and develop specific segments of the architecture

- Effective architecture re-use requires modular architecture segments that can be taken and incorporated into broader architectures and solutions

It is impractical to present a definitive partitioning model for architecture. Each enterprise needs to adopt a partitioning model that reflects its own operating model. The TOGAF standard includes classification criteria that can be applied when partitioning architectures, and guidance for activities within the Preliminary Phase for establishing a partition.

Steps within the Preliminary Phase to support architecture partitioning are as follows:
- Determine the organization structure for architecture within the enterprise
- Determine the responsibilities for each standing architecture team
- Determine the relationships between architectures

Once the Preliminary Phase is complete, the teams conducting the architecture should be understood. Each team should have a defined scope and the relationships between teams and architecture should be understood. Allocation of teams to architecture scope is illustrated in Figure 17.

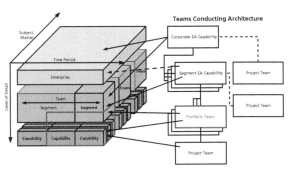

Figure 17: Allocation of Teams to Architecture Scope

6.3 Architecture Repository

Supporting the Enterprise Continuum is the concept of an Architecture Repository which can be used to store different classes of architectural output at different levels of abstraction, created by the ADM. By means of the Enterprise Continuum and Architecture Repository, architects are encouraged to leverage all other relevant architectural resources when developing an Organization-Specific Architecture.

In this context, the TOGAF ADM can be regarded as describing a process lifecycle that operates at multiple levels within the organization, operating within a holistic governance framework and producing aligned outputs that reside in an Architecture Repository. The Enterprise Continuum provides a valuable context for understanding architectural models: it shows building blocks and their relationships to each other, and the constraints and requirements on a cycle of architecture development.

The structure of the TOGAF Architecture Repository is shown in Figure 18.

The major components within an Architecture Repository are as follows:

- The **Architecture Metamodel** describes the organizationally tailored application of an architecture framework, including a metamodel for architecture content
- The **Architecture Capability** defines the parameters, structures, and processes that support governance of the Architecture Repository
- The **Architecture Landscape** shows an architectural view of the building blocks that are in use within the organization today (e.g., a list of the live applications); the landscape is likely to exist at multiple levels of abstraction to suit different architecture objectives
- The **Standards Information Base** (SIB) captures the standards with which new architectures must comply, which may include industry standards, selected products and services from suppliers, or shared services already deployed within the organization

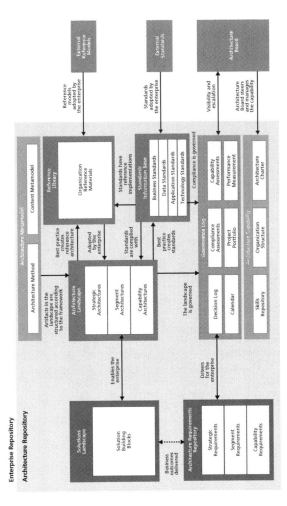

Figure 18: TOGAF Architecture Repository Structure

- The **Reference Library** provides guidelines, templates, patterns, and other forms of reference material that can be leveraged in order to accelerate the creation of new architectures for the enterprise
- The **Governance Log** provides a record of governance activity across the enterprise
- The **Architecture Requirements Repository** provides a view of all authorized architecture requirements which have been agreed with the Architecture Board
- The **Solutions Landscape** presents an architectural representation of the SBBs supporting the Architecture Landscape which have been planned or deployed by the enterprise

6.3.1 The Enterprise Repository

The Architecture Repository is one part of the wider Enterprise Repository. While the Architecture Repository holds information concerning the Enterprise Architecture and associated artifacts, there are a considerable number of enterprise repositories that support the architecture. These can include development repositories, specific operating environments, instructions, and configuration management repositories.

Chapter 7
Architecture Capability Framework

This chapter introduces the Architecture Capability Framework.

Part VI of the standard: Architecture Capability Framework provides a set of reference materials for how to establish an architecture function within an enterprise.

A summary of the contents of Part VI is shown in Table 17.

Table 17: TOGAF Part VI Contents Summary

Chapter	Description
Establishing an Architecture Capability	Guidelines on how to use the ADM to establish an Architecture Capability within an organization.
Architecture Board	Guidelines for establishing and operating an Enterprise Architecture Board.
Architecture Compliance	Guidelines for ensuring project compliance to architecture.
Architecture Contracts	Guidelines for defining and using Architecture Contracts.
Architecture Governance	Framework and guidelines for Architecture Governance.
Architecture Maturity Models	Techniques for evaluating and quantifying an organization's maturity in Enterprise Architecture.
Architecture Skills Framework	A set of role, skill, and experience norms for staff undertaking Enterprise Architecture work

An overall structure for an Architecture Capability Framework is shown in Figure 19.

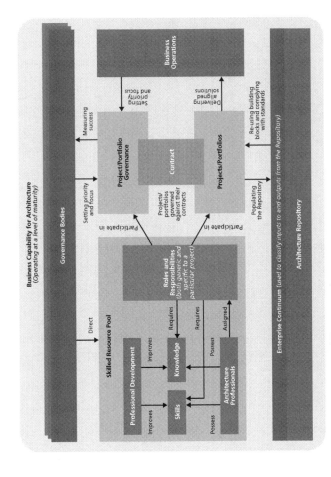

Figure 19: Architecture Capability Framework

7.1 Establishing an Architecture Capability

Implementing any capability within an organization requires the design of the four domain architectures: Business, Data, Application, and Technology. Establishing the architecture practice within an organization therefore requires the design of:

- The Business Architecture of the architecture practice, which highlights the Architecture Governance, architecture processes, architecture organizational structure, architecture information requirements, architecture products, etc.
- The Data Architecture, which defines the structure of the organization's Enterprise Continuum and Architecture Repository
- The Application Architecture, which specifies the functionality and/or applications services required to enable the architecture practice
- The Technology Architecture, which specifies the architecture practice's infrastructure requirements in support of the architecture applications and Enterprise Continuum

7.2 Architecture Governance

The Architecture Capability Framework contains a framework and guidelines for Architecture Governance. Architecture Governance is the practice by which Enterprise Architectures and other architectures are managed and controlled at an enterprise-wide level. It includes the following:

- Implementing a system of controls over the creation and monitoring of all architecture components and activities, to ensure the effective introduction, implementation, and evolution of architectures within the organization
- Implementing a system to ensure compliance with internal and external standards and regulatory obligations
- Establishing processes that support effective management of the above processes within agreed parameters
- Establishing and documenting decision structures that influence the Enterprise Architecture; this includes stakeholders that provide input to decisions

- Developing practices that ensure accountability to a clearly identified stakeholder community, both inside and outside the organization

7.3 Architecture Board

An Enterprise Architecture is more than just the artifacts produced by the application of the ADM process. Making the organization act according to the principles laid down in the architecture requires a decision-making framework. The Architecture Capability Framework provides a set of guidelines for establishing and operating an Enterprise Architecture Board. An Architecture Board is responsible for operational items and must be capable of making decisions in situations of possible conflict and be accountable for taking those decisions. It should therefore be a representation of all the key stakeholders in the architecture, and will typically comprise a group of executives responsible for the review and maintenance of the overall architecture. It is important that the members of the Architecture Board cover architecture, business, and program management areas.

Issues for which the Architecture Board can be made responsible and accountable are:
- Providing the basis for all decision-making with regard to changes to the architectures
- Consistency between sub-architectures
- Identifying re-usable components
- Flexibility of Enterprise Architecture; to meet business needs and utilize new technologies
- Enforcement of architecture compliance
- Improving the maturity level of architecture discipline within the organization
- Ensuring that the discipline of architecture-based development is adopted
- Supporting a visible escalation capability for out-of-bounds decisions

The Architecture Board is also responsible for operational items, such as the monitoring and control of Architecture Contracts (see Section 3.29), and for governance items, such as producing usable governance materials. Important tasks are:

- Assigning architectural tasks
- Formally approving architectural products
- Resolving architectural conflicts

7.4 Architecture Compliance

Using architecture to structure IT development in an organization implies that IT projects should comply with the architecture roadmap. If that's not the case, then there must be a good reason for it.

To determine whether this is the case, an Architecture Compliance strategy should be adopted with specific measures to ensure compliance with the architecture. The Architecture Capability Framework includes a set of processes, guidelines, and a checklist for ensuring project compliance to the architecture, including:

- Project Impact Assessments that illustrate how the Enterprise Architecture impacts on the major projects within an organization
- The Architecture Compliance Review process (see Figure 20), which is a formal process for reviewing the compliance of projects to the Enterprise Architecture

7.5 Architecture Skills Framework

The Architecture Capability Framework provides a set of role, skill, and experience norms for staff undertaking Enterprise Architecture work.

"Enterprise Architecture" and "Enterprise Architect" are widely used but poorly defined terms in the IT industry today. They are used to denote a variety of practices and skills applied in a wide variety of architecture domains. There is a need for better classification to enable more implicit understanding of what type of architect/architecture is being described.

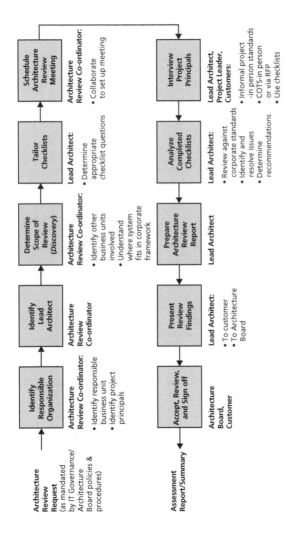

Figure 20: Architecture Compliance Review Process

This lack of uniformity leads to difficulties for organizations seeking to recruit or assign/promote staff to fill positions in the architecture field. Because of the different usages of terms, there is often misunderstanding and miscommunication between those seeking to recruit for, and those seeking to fill, the various roles of the architect.

The TOGAF Architecture Skills Framework attempts to address this need by providing definitions of the architecting skills and proficiency levels required of personnel, internal or external, who are to perform the various architecting roles defined within the TOGAF framework.

Skill categories include:
- Generic Skills, typically comprising leadership, team-working, inter-personal skills, etc.
- Business Skills & Methods, typically comprising business cases, business process, strategic planning, etc.
- Enterprise Architecture Skills, typically comprising modeling, building block design, applications and role design, systems integration, etc.
- Program or Project Management Skills, typically comprising managing business change, project management methods and tools, etc.
- IT General Knowledge Skills, typically comprising brokering applications, asset management, migration planning, SLAs, etc.
- Technical IT Skills, typically comprising software engineering, security, data interchange, data management, etc.
- Legal Environment, typically comprising data protection laws, contract law, procurement law, fraud, etc.

Appendix A
Migration Summary

This appendix contains high-level migration information – a summary description of what is changed between Version 9.1 and Version 9.2 of the TOGAF Standard.

A.1 Changes between Version 9.1 and Version 9.2 of the TOGAF Standard

Version 9.1	Version 9.2	Comments
Part I: Introduction	Part I: Introduction	
1: Introduction	1: Introduction	The introduction is revised to describe this update and in particular to introduce the TOGAF Library. The document set description is changed from seven to six parts (Reference Models are now relocated to the TOGAF Library). A description of the structure of the TOGAF Library is added. In the Executive Overview, the descriptions of "enterprise" and the "enterprise operating model" are refined. The descriptions are also updated to place an emphasis on "Digital Transformation". The end sections from TOGAF 9.1 Chapter 4 are moved to the end of Chapter 1, and provide information on Using the TOGAF Standard and Why Join The Open Group.

Version 9.1	Version 9.2	Comments
2: Core Concepts	2: Core Concepts	References to ISO/IEC/IEEE 42010 are updated here and throughout the document to the 2011 edition. The structure of the Architecture Repository is updated to include the Solutions Landscape and Architecture Requirements Repository. A reference to the IT4IT Reference Architecture is added as an example of adopting other elements to integrate with when tailoring the TOGAF framework. Minor editorial cleanup is applied to this (and all chapters).
3: Definitions	3: Definitions	The following new terms are added: Application Component, Architecture Model, Business Capability, Business Model, Course of Action, Information System Service, Model Kind, Organization Map, Service, Service Portfolio, Technology Component, Technology Service, Value Stream, Viewpoint Library The following terms are deleted: Application Platform Interface, Constraint, Methodology, Model, Performance Management, Platform The following terms are revised: Actor, Architecture Domain, Architectural Style, Architecture, Architecture Development Method, Architecture Framework, Architecture Governance, Boundaryless Information Flow, Building Block, Business Architecture, Concern, Service Orientation, Service-Oriented Architecture, Stakeholder View and Viewpoint are renamed to Architecture View and Architecture Viewpoint. Concerns is renamed to Concern.

Version 9.1	Version 9.2	Comments
4: Release Notes	Removed	This chapter is removed. Details of the release updates will be published in a separate White Paper. Partial contents (4.5, 4.6) about using the TOGAF standard are updated and moved to end of Chapter 1.
Part II: Architecture Development Method	**Part II: Architecture Development Method**	
5: Introduction	4: Introduction to Part II	The description of supporting guidelines and techniques is updated to also include the TOGAF Library. The IT4IT Reference Architecture is added to the examples.
6: Preliminary Phase	5: Preliminary Phase	The Approach section is moved to the end of the chapter. The TOGAF Library is named as an input. The step "Implement architecture tools" is now renamed to "Develop strategy and implementation plans for tools and techniques", and additional guidance provided. Terminology tailoring now recommends creation of an Enterprise Glossary.
7: Phase A: Architecture Vision	6: Phase A: Architecture Vision	The Approach section is moved to the end of the chapter and revised extensively. One of the steps is renamed from "Evaluate business capabilities" to "Evaluate capabilities". Explicit mention of a Stakeholder Map is added into the Develop the Architecture Vision step. Guidance is added on evaluation of business models and identification of required business capabilities. New artifacts added: Business Model diagram, Business Capability map, Value Stream map

Version 9.1	Version 9.2	Comments
8: Phase B: Business Architecture	7: Phase B: Business Architecture	The Approach section is moved to the end of the chapter and revised extensively to include further advice on Business Architecture. The first objective is revised to address the Statement of Architecture Work (rather than the Request for Architecture Work as it stated previously). Artifacts added: Value Stream catalog, Business Capabilities catalog, Value Stream Stages catalog, Value Stream/Capability matrix, Strategy/Capability matrix, Capability/Organization matrix, Business model diagram, Business Capability map, Value Stream map, Organization map
9: Phase C: Information Systems Architectures	8: Phase C: Information Systems Architectures	The phase text is simplified to just Objectives and Approach, with pointers to the following two chapters for details.
10: Phase C: Information Systems Architectures – Data Architecture	9: Phase C: Information Systems Architectures – Data Architecture	The first objective is revised to address the Statement of Architecture Work (rather than the Request for Architecture Work as it stated previously). The Approach section is moved to the end of the chapter with a minor revision to example standards.
11: Phase C: Information Systems Architectures – Application Architecture	10: Phase C: Information Systems Architectures – Application Architecture	The first objective is revised to address the Statement of Architecture Work (rather than the Request for Architecture Work as it stated previously). The Approach section is moved to the end of the chapter with minor revisions. In Steps, to support agile development a "must" is changed to a "should" (as in should complete all steps).

Version 9.1	Version 9.2	Comments
12: Phase D: Technology Architecture	11: Phase D: Technology Architecture	The first objective is revised to address the Statement of Architecture Work (rather than the Request for Architecture Work as it stated previously). It is also refined to focus on building block delivery through technology components and services. The Approach section is moved to the end of the chapter with revisions to address emerging technologies and Digital Transformation. References to the TRM and III-RM reference models are updated to refer to the TOGAF Series Guides.
13: Phase E: Opportunities & Solutions	12: Phase E: Opportunities & Solutions	An objective is added to define the Solution Building Blocks to finalize the Target Architecture. The Approach section is moved to the end of the chapter with minor revisions.
14: Phase F: Migration Planning	13: Phase F: Migration Planning	The Approach section is moved to the end of the chapter with minor revisions.
15: Phase G: Implementation Governance	14: Phase G: Implementation Governance	The Approach section is moved to the end of the chapter with minor revisions.
16: Phase H: Architecture Change Management	15: Phase H: Architecture Change Management	The Approach section is moved to the end of the chapter.

Version 9.1	Version 9.2	Comments
17: ADM Architecture Requirements Management	16: ADM Architecture Requirements Management	The Approach section is moved to the end of the chapter. References to the "Requirements Repository" are changed to the "Architecture Requirements Repository".
Part III: ADM Guidelines and Techniques	Part III: ADM Guidelines and Techniques	
18: Introduction	17: Introduction to Part III	References are added to external guides for examples of architectural style: Security and SOA. Additional text is provided about architectural styles including example documents. Minor editorials are also applied.
19: Applying Iteration to the ADM	18: Applying Iteration to the ADM	Minor editorial changes only. No substantive changes.
20: Applying the ADM across the Architecture Landscape	19: Applying the ADM across the Architecture Landscape	Minor editorial changes only. No substantive changes.
21: Security Architecture and the ADM	Removed	This chapter is removed and advice on risk and security is published separately as: Integrating Risk and Security within a TOGAF® Enterprise Architecture; available at: www.opengroup.org/library/g152
22: Using TOGAF to Define & Govern SOAs	Removed	This chapter is removed. Content now published as: TOGAF® Series Guide: Using the TOGAF® Framework to Define and Govern Service-Oriented Architectures; available at: www.opengroup.org/library/g174
23: Architecture Principles	20: Architecture Principles	Minor editorial changes only. No substantive changes.

Version 9.1	Version 9.2	Comments
24: Stakeholder Management	21: Stakeholder Management	The example stakeholder map has been updated to include the new Business Architecture artifacts.
25: Architecture Patterns	22: Architecture Patterns	The introduction has been updated. The examples in Sections 25.1.4, 25.2, and 25.3 have been removed, as they are no longer available. Minor editorial changes applied.
26: Business Scenarios and Business Goals	Removed	This chapter is removed and published separately as: TOGAF® Series Guide: Business Scenarios; available at: www.opengroup.org/library/g176
27: Gap Analysis	23: Gap Analysis	Text is updated to refer to the TOGAF TRM rather than the Technical Reference Model. Minor editorials. No substantive changes.
28: Migration Planning Techniques	24: Migration Planning Techniques	Rather than referring directly to the TOGAF TRM, the text is updated to now refer to services from the defined taxonomy in the enterprise.
29: Inter-operability Requirements	25: Interoperability Requirements	The end Summary section is removed. Otherwise no substantive changes.
30: Business Transformation Readiness Assessment	26: Business Transformation Readiness Assessment	Minor editorial changes only. No substantive changes.

Version 9.1	Version 9.2	Comments
31: Risk Management	27: Risk Management	Minor editorial changes only. No substantive changes.
32: Capability-Based Planning	28: Capability-Based Planning	Minor editorial changes only. No substantive changes.
Part IV: Architecture Content Framework	**Part IV: Architecture Content Framework**	
33: Introduction	29: Introduction to Part IV	The Content Metamodel Overview figure is updated. In the Business Architecture, the Function category is changed to Behavior. Business Capabilities, Course of Action, and Value Streams are added to Behavior. Location is moved from the Organization category in Business Architecture to Architecture Requirements (as Locations). In the Technology Architecture, Platform Services are changed to Technology Services. Minor editorial changes.
34: Content Metamodel	30: Content Metamodel	The descriptions of the concepts of Catalog, Matrix, and Diagram are moved to Chapter 35. Platform Services are renamed Technology Services. The following entities are added to the metamodel: Business Capability, Course of Action, Value Stream The list of artifacts by phase is removed from this chapter. The changes to the metamodel for extensions are now referred to as Extensions. The metamodel diagrams and the metamodel relationships tables are revised. New relationships are added, and others have been changed. Changes have been made for consistency across the diagrams and relationships table.

Version 9.1	Version 9.2	Comments
		The Location entity is now a global entity, so text about it being added as part of the Infrastructure Consolidation extension is removed. Figures now show it as a white core element. The Communications and Engineering diagram is renamed to the Network and Communications diagram.
35: Architectural Artifacts	31: Architectural Artifacts	Terminology and conceptual figure updated for ISO/IEC/IEEE 42010:2011 and ISO/IEC/IEEE 15288:2015. The description of catalogs, matrices, and diagrams is moved from Chapter 34 to this chapter. Additional artifacts are added: Business Model diagram, Business Capability map, Value Stream map, Business Capabilities catalog, Value Stream catalog, Value Stream Stages catalog, Value Stream/Capability matrix, Strategy/Capability matrix, Capability/Organization matrix, Organization map The Communications and Engineering diagram is renamed to the Network and Communications diagram. The obsolete Section 35.7 is removed.
36: Architecture Deliverables	32: Architecture Deliverables	The description of tailoring changes has been changed from project and process management frameworks to simply management frameworks. Minor editorial changes. No substantive changes.
37: Building Blocks	33: Building Blocks	Minor change to building block definition.

Version 9.1	Version 9.2	Comments
Part V: Enterprise Continuum & Tools	Part V: Enterprise Continuum & Tools	
38: Introduction	34: Introduction to Part V	Minor editorial changes only. No substantive changes.
39: Enterprise Continuum	35: Enterprise Continuum	Minor updates to position the TOGAF TRM as an example. References to the TRM and III-RM are now moved to external TOGAF Series Guides and the TOGAF Library. The IT4IT Reference Architecture is added as an example.
40: Architecture Partitioning	36: Architecture Partitioning	Minor editorial changes only. No substantive changes.
41: Architecture Repository	37: Architecture Repository	The Architecture Requirements Repository and the Solutions Landscape are added to the Architecture Repository. The IT4IT Reference Architecture is added as an example reference architecture. The list of example external reference models is removed.
42: Tools for Architecture Development	38: Tools for Architecture Development	Minor editorial changes only. No substantive changes.
Part VI: TOGAF Reference Models	Removed	
43: Foundation Architecture: Technical Reference Model	Removed	Content moved to: TOGAF® Series Guide: The TOGAF Technical Reference Model (TRM); available at: www.opengroup.org/library/g175 Existing Part VI removed.

Version 9.1	Version 9.2	Comments
44: Integrated Information Infrastructure Reference Model	Removed	Content moved to: TOGAF® Series Guide: The TOGAF Integrated Information Infrastructure Reference Model (III RM): An Architected Approach to Boundaryless Information Flow™; available at: www.opengroup.org/library/g179
Part VII: Architecture Capability Framework	**Part VI: Architecture Capability Framework**	
45: Introduction	39: Introduction to Part VI	Minor editorial changes only. No substantive changes.
46: Establishing an Architecture Capability	40: Establishing an Architecture Capability	Minor editorial changes only. No substantive changes.
47: Architecture Board	41: Architecture Board	Minor editorial changes only. No substantive changes.
48: Architecture Compliance	42: Architecture Compliance	Minor editorial changes only. No substantive changes.
49: Architecture Contracts	43: Architecture Contracts	Minor editorial changes only. No substantive changes.
50. Architecture Governance	44: Architecture Governance	Reference to the White Paper: Mapping between TOGAF 8.1 and COBIT 4.0 is removed. Minor editorial changes also applied.
51: Architecture Maturity Models	45: Architecture Maturity Models	The text referencing "ACMM Version 1.2" is removed. Level 5: Optimizing has been changed to Level 5: Measured.
52: Architecture Skills Framework	46: Architecture Skills Framework	Minor editorial changes only. No substantive changes.

Version 9.1	Version 9.2	Comments
Appendices	Appendices	
A: Glossary of Supplementary Definitions	A: Glossary of Supplementary Definitions	Definition of System aligned to ISO/IEC/IEEE 15288:2015. Removal of supplementary terms no longer used in the document, or those moved to the Definitions chapter (e.g., Application Component, Information System Service, Service, Technology Component). Minor consistency changes.
B: Abbreviations	B: Abbreviations	Minor changes.

Appendix B
TOGAF Reference Models

This appendix provides a brief introduction to two TOGAF Reference Models provided in the TOGAF Library.

B.1 TOGAF Foundation Architecture

The TOGAF Foundation Architecture is an architecture that provides a foundation on which specific architectures and architectural components can be built. This Foundation Architecture is embodied in the Technical Reference Model (TRM). The TRM is universally applicable and therefore can be used to build any system architecture.

Technical Reference Model (TRM)

The TRM, shown in Figure 21, is a model and taxonomy of generic platform services. The taxonomy defines the terminology and provides a coherent description of its components. Its purpose is to give a

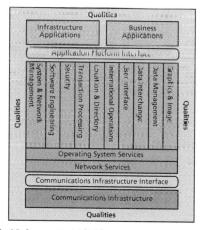

Figure 21: Technical Reference Model (TRM)

conceptual description of an Information System. The TRM model is a graphical representation of the taxonomy to act as an aid for understanding.

B.2 Integrated Information Infrastructure Reference Model (III-RM)

Whereas the Foundation Architecture describes a typical application platform environment, the second reference model included in the Enterprise Continuum, the Integrated Information Infrastructure Reference Model (III-RM), focuses on the application software space. The III-RM is a "Common Systems Architecture" in Enterprise Continuum terms.

The III-RM is shown in and is a subset of the TOGAF TRM in terms of its overall scope, but it also expands certain parts of the TRM, in particular in the business applications and infrastructure applications parts.

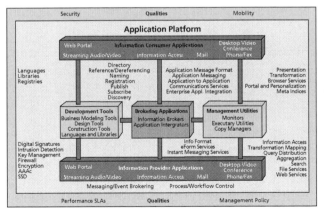

Figure 22: The III-RM in Detail

Glossary

Application Architecture

A description of the structure and interaction of the applications as groups of capabilities that provide key business functions and manage the data assets.

Architecture

1. The fundamental concepts or properties of a system in its environment embodied in its elements, relationships, and in the principles of its design and evolution.
2. The structure of components, their inter-relationships, and the principles and guidelines governing their design and evolution over time.

Architecture Building Block (ABB)

A constituent of the architecture model that describes a single aspect of the overall model.

Architecture Continuum

A part of the Enterprise Continuum. A repository of architectural elements with increasing detail and specialization.

Architecture Development Method (ADM)

The core of the TOGAF framework. A multi-phase, iterative approach to develop and use an Enterprise Architecture to shape and govern business transformation and implementation projects.

Architecture Framework

A conceptual structure used to plan, develop, implement, govern, and sustain an architecture.

Architecture Principle

A qualitative statement of intent that should be met by the architecture.

Architecture View

A representation of a system from the perspective of a related set of concerns.

Architecture Viewpoint

A specification of the conventions for a particular kind of architecture view.

Baseline

A specification that has been formally reviewed and agreed upon, that thereafter serves as the basis for further development or change and that can be changed only through formal change control procedures or a type of procedure such as configuration management.

Business Architecture

A representation of holistic, multi-dimensional business views of: capabilities, end-to-end value delivery, information, and organizational structure; and the relationships among these business views and strategies, products, policies, initiatives, and stakeholders.

Capability

An ability that an organization, person, or system possesses.

Capability Architecture

A highly detailed description of the architectural approach to realize a particular solution or solution aspect.

Capability Increment

A discrete portion of a capability architecture that delivers specific value. When all increments have been completed, the capability has been realized.

Data Architecture
A description of the structure and interaction of the enterprise's major types and sources of data, logical data assets, physical data assets, and data management resources.

Enterprise
The highest level (typically) of description of an organization and typically covers all missions and functions. An enterprise will often span multiple organizations.

Enterprise Continuum
A categorization mechanism useful for classifying architecture and solution artifacts, both internal and external to the Architecture Repository, as they evolve from generic Foundation Architectures to Organization-Specific Architectures.

Foundation Architecture
Generic building blocks, their inter-relationships with other building blocks, combined with the principles and guidelines that provide a foundation on which more specific architectures can be built.

Framework
A structure for content or process that can be used as a tool to structure thinking, ensuring consistency and completeness.

Gap
A statement of difference between two states. Used in the context of gap analysis, where the difference between the Baseline and Target Architecture is identified.

Governance
The discipline of monitoring, managing, and steering a business (or IS/IT landscape) to deliver the business outcome required.

Metamodel

A model that describes how and with what the architecture will be described in a structured way.

Repository

A system that manages all of the data of an enterprise, including data and process models and other enterprise information.

Requirement

A statement of need that must be met by a particular architecture or work package.

Risk Management

The management of risks and issues that may threaten the success of the Enterprise Architecture practice and its ability to meet is vision, goals, and objectives, and, importantly, its service provision.

Segment Architecture

A detailed, formal description of areas within an enterprise, used at the program or portfolio level to organize and align change activity.

Service

A repeatable activity; a discrete behavior that a building block may be requested or otherwise triggered to perform.

Service Orientation

Viewing an enterprise, system, or building block in terms of services provided and consumed.

Service Oriented Architecture (SOA)

An architectural style that supports service orientation.

Solution Architecture

A description of a discrete and focused business operation or activity and how IS/IT supports that operation.

Solution Building Block (SBB)

A candidate solution which conforms to the specification of an Architecture Building Block (ABB).

Solutions Continuum

A part of the Enterprise Continuum. A repository of re-usable solutions for future implementation efforts. It contains implementations of the corresponding definitions in the Architecture Continuum.

Stakeholder

An individual, team, organization, or class thereof, having an interest in a system.

Target Architecture

The description of a future state of the architecture being developed for an organization.

Technical Reference Model (TRM)

A structure which allows the components of an information system to be described in a consistent manner.

Technology Architecture

A description of the structure and interaction of the technology services, and logical and physical technology components.

Transition Architecture

A formal description of one state of the architecture at an architecturally significant point in time.

Value Stream
A representation of an end-to-end collection of value-adding activities that create an overall result for a customer, stakeholder, or end user.

View
See Architecture View.

Viewpoint
See Architecture Viewpoint.

Work Package
A set of actions identified to achieve one or more objectives for the business. A work package can be a part of a project, a complete project, or a program.

Index